Daniel Quick
Barry Kelly

The
Customer
Education
Playbook

How Leading Companies
Engage, Convert, and
Retain Customers

WILEY

Dedicated to the Thought Industries team, our customers, and the broader customer education community.

Contents

Contents

Introduction

In today's subscription economy, your business is unlikely to survive if your customers aren't gaining value from your products. This is a sound argument for developing great products, of course, but that's not enough. After all, how can customers gain value from something they don't know how to effectively use? For your customers to achieve their desired outcomes, you must teach them what they need to know. Enter *customer education,* a rapidly evolving field that focuses on teaching customers the right things, at the right time, so that they find value from your products and become advocates of your brand. An educated customer is a satisfied customer that delivers long-term value to your business.

Here's a secret. Customers are always learning, and they are learning at every stage of their lifecycle. Whether they are learning how to solve their problem, why your solution is better than others, or how to develop mastery with your product, customers are being educated and educating themselves, for better or for worse. Left to their own devices, customers will often struggle through this learning process; many will fail to adopt your product, much less become masters of it. Without a customer education strategy, learning will happen anyway – just not the kind that positively impacts your business. You don't want customers learning the wrong things; that your product is "difficult to use," for example, or "doesn't offer value to someone like me."

Whether you think you are or not, you're probably already investing in customer education. If you're putting money into content marketing, account managers, or customer support – you're educating your customers.

The question is, are you educating them *successfully*? Are you simply reacting to events as they occur, or are you able to plan ahead so that you can proactively empower your customers at each stage and optimize your business for scale?

At Thought Industries, we are seeing more and more companies looking to create a more strategic plan for their customer education. After all, companies who are leaders in their categories, like Salesforce, Gainsight, HubSpot, Motorola, and 3M, all invested early in customer education as a way to maximize and scale lifetime value, and this paints a compelling picture. There is an immense amount of untapped value lying unclaimed on the table.

However, that doesn't mean that developing a customer education strategy is easy. As a new field, practitioners often lack prior experience, and there are very few resources to help them achieve success in their roles. They can't even reliably look for guidance from their managers, who – lacking experience themselves – will usually expect customer education specialists to simply "figure it out." In this reality, how can new customer education functions (1) form and pitch their strategies; (2) effectively communicate their goals; (3) identify the optimal formats for their content; and (4) distribute, measure, and monetize the training they create?

These early-stage challenges are so great that many organizations find themselves caught in a sort of inertia. According to our *2020 State of the Customer Training Report,* 96 percent of companies believe that customer training is important to their organization. The value of training is not in question here. However, almost half stated that they are struggling to measure the impact of training programs, and only 14 percent believe a majority of their customers are adequately trained.

With our finger on the pulse of the industry, and a combined 50 years in the industry, we recognize that educating customers might be essential, but that doesn't make it straightforward, especially as no two customers are the same. They are all learners, but they all need something different. Effective customer education requires an investment. Yes, that means investing in technology for delivering engaging customer learning rather than relying on a traditional, internal-facing learning management system (LMS) that is more suited for employee and corporate training. However, more importantly, we've seen how essential it is to invest in a cohesive, central strategy that pulls all the different elements of a successful program together.

The Customer Education Playbook: How Leading Companies Engage, Convert, and Retain Customers, the bulk of which comprehensively discusses a framework we call the *Customer Education Playbook,* will help you develop that strategy. In Chapters 1–2, we'll define customer education and discuss how to operationalize it in your business, whether you're just getting started or hoping to mature your program. In Chapters 3–14, we'll cover the 12 steps of the *Customer Education Playbook,* all of which are based on research conducted from speaking to hundreds of customer education professionals and executives across multiple B2B industries. Finally, in Chapters 15 and 16, we'll explore the phases to achieving a mature customer education function and give you our thoughts on the future of the industry.

Our hope is that the *Customer Education Playbook* will help professionals on the ground to develop a clear and structured approach that leads to impactful, engaging, and measurable customer education programs. As you read the following chapters, you'll learn the answers to all of those questions you've previously been expected to "figure out on your own," and you will get practical and actionable advice on how to effectively target and educate your customers – transforming them from prospects to champions.

1

How Customer Education Transforms Prospects to Champions

Your customers are the center of your universe. The survival of your business hinges on their choices – whether they buy or churn, renew their subscription, tell their friends about you, or become a drain on your support teams.

As the center of your universe, your customers deserve your research, your dedication, your focus, and a deep level of understanding into their behavior at every stage of their journey.

The Evolution of Customer Education

The emphasis on "Customer is King" is far from a new idea, but over the past decade, there has been a slow shift toward understanding how important it is not only to know the customer but also to educate them. This evolution has been accelerated with drivers from three directions.

1. *The increasing complexity of today's products.* Today, customers need more hand-holding than ever to get to the point of value with your product. If you don't educate them on how they can reach that value quickly, they may assume that your product isn't a good fit or that it's too complex for their needs.

2. *More competition than ever before.* According to US Census data, new business formation has been growing steadily since 2010, and between 2019 and 2020, the number of new businesses registered leapt by 24 percent.[1] A well-executed customer education strategy can make all the difference in helping your business stand out from the competition.

3. *Growing customer expectations.* Education and training have become an expected part of the customer experience. Whether it's in-product tutorials, skills-based learning, or certifications, your customers want to learn and grow as professionals and are increasingly looking to you to make it happen.

The Business Benefits of Education Across the Lifecycle

The focus on educating the customer may have started out as the route to customer success, but what began with an emphasis on improving customer experience has quickly proved itself to be an economic imperative, an approach that pays dividends across the customer lifecycle.

Pre-sale

The concept of an Educated Qualified Lead (EQL) is simple – a lead that is already knowledgeable about your product and what it can do for them before they reach out to show curiosity or interest. By educating the market, generating leads becomes easier, and the quality of those leads is much improved, with many ready to move into the second phase of the sales cycle even before they reach out. These inbound prospects that come

---

[1] US Census Bureau, "Business Formation Statistics," December 8, 2021, https://www.census.gov/econ/bfs/index.html.

through your door already have some idea of what gap you can fill for them, and therefore they can ask better questions and already have a foundation for learning.

Your interested customers have now become true prospects, and at this stage you might be channeling them into some kind of trial. Customer education offers a route to optimizing trials for success by focusing on the value proposition and controlling the flow of information so that customers don't feel overwhelmed. Examples might include offering the customer a tool to learn new vocabulary at the start, using visual aids to shape thinking, or breaking down the trial into smaller sections where customers can really kick the tires. The trial stage is a really sensitive moment in the customer journey, and customer education allows you to curate experiences that work for individual personas and roles. You can also extend the benefits of education to your channel partners, from distributors to resellers. The quicker and easier you can get these important stakeholders trained and confident with your product, the more likely that they will achieve results on your behalf and the less you will need to micromanage those relationships behind the scenes.

Education also allows you to scale and streamline your trial and onboarding processes far beyond what you could achieve with customer success managers (CSMs) and sales teams alone. If your prospects can walk themselves through a trial experience or an onboarding journey, complete with tutorials and education built for any points of friction, you are immediately reducing your customer acquisition costs (CAC) while increasing the number of simultaneous customers that you can onboard.

Post-sale

Congratulations! Your prospects have become customers. They've signed on the dotted line, onboarded your product, and passed the line into a post-sale relationship. But don't make the mistake of seeing that line as a finish line – in reality, it's more like your starting point. At this stage, marketing and sales often drop out of the relationship, and the baton is regularly passed over to customer support or customer success. Without a strong educational strategy in place for proactive support, CS teams can become a reactive presence, waiting for problems and troubleshooting as they occur.

While you can use your CSMs to train or support a single customer easily, once you hit a certain threshold, it becomes much more difficult to scale. How can a single CSM effectively manage training for many customers, all of whom will be at different stages of adoption with your product, and still have time to build relationships and drive value? Moreover, what happens when CSMs leave your organization and you haven't yet trained new ones to manage accounts? As your growth relies on deeper product adoption and customer satisfaction, you need a scalable path to customer onboarding so that they realize value as quickly as possible and can access the help they need on their own terms.

Customer education can be used to deflect support tickets and even turn support interactions into training interventions at the moment of need. Instead of onboarding new CSMs to handle an ever-increasing number of tickets, you can strategically place education where known pain points occur in your product, or you can develop a robust knowledge base so that customers can resolve their own problems. As customers become more confident that they will find the answers, your support costs drop, even as the number of customers you onboard increases.

Advocacy

Your customers are now achieving increasing levels of comfort and mastery with your product, and they're getting there faster than ever, speeding up overall time to value (TTV). Providing opportunities for customers to gain deeper mastery will lead to an increase in net promoter scores (NPS) and customer satisfaction (CSAT), because you're creating brand ambassadors who have used your product to become more effective in their role. The more legitimacy you gain in the market as an expert in your field, the more opportunities there are to grow direct revenues through paid education, such as courses and paid eLearning.

Today, skills-based learning and certifications are highly relevant and increasingly in demand. Customers are happy to pay for applicable and significant credentials that bolster their resume. Companies who can leverage this and create certifications that become known as the industry standard are carving out a competitive advantage, alongside a new line of revenue.

Crossing the Chasm: When Is the Right Time to Invest in Customer Education?

One of the first questions that you'll likely ask yourself is: When is the right time for your business to start investing in customer education?

To answer this question, we want to touch on the idea of the *Technology Adoption Lifecycle* by Geoffrey Moore,[2] as seen in Figure 1.1.

As your customers move through the lifecycle, they expect an increasing amount from your company. Innovators and early adopters, by nature, are likely to be more enthusiastic and self-motivated to learn and play with your product. On the business side, you have a lot more time on your hands at this stage to offer a white-glove experience when they need support. In contrast, as you cross the chasm into early-majority and late-majority

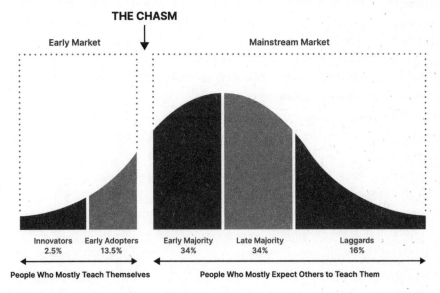

Figure 1.1 Crossing the Chasm

---

[2] Geoffrey Moore, *Crossing the Chasm: Marketing and Selling Disruptive Products to Mainstream Customers,* 3rd Edition (New York: Harper Collins Publishers, 2014).

adopters, your customers will start to expect more hand-holding and an established strategy for training them in how to be successful with your product. The profile of these kinds of customers dictates that they are going to be less comfortable or successful going it alone.

Conventionally, as companies feel this pressure – the need for customer education becomes clear. When you arrive at this point, as you cross the chasm, your business will need to have a sound strategy in place for education if it is going to successfully scale.

Let's take this even further and highlight the benefits of creating this strategy earlier in your maturity. As already outlined, customer education is beneficial throughout the customer journey, so why not bring it in at the beginning of your business maturity? Don't just view education as a function that will solve the learning needs of late-majority customers when they ask for help. Rather, also leverage education as a scaling function for content marketing and lead generation, as well as to support early adopters who might not traditionally need education as much but for whom low-effort content such as short, engaging videos can really deepen their engagement with the product. In that way, education helps your company to move from early market to mainstream, effectively facilitating the crossing of the chasm rather than merely reacting to it.

This attitude may sound like we're conflating education with the marketing function of the business – and that's okay! There is a lot of overlap between the two. If the goal of marketing is to drive awareness and to attract and convert new customers, customer education can play a big role in that if you start your education function early. It's never too soon to be thinking about your customer learning strategy and journey, identifying the moments of their customer lifecycle and crafting a content strategy around teaching the right education at each of those moments. Increasingly, customers expect production-quality education, thanks to the likes of YouTube, TikTok, Instagram, and more, so getting education involved in marketing projects can be a great way to boost marketing campaigns, too.

Ready to get started? In the next chapter, we will discuss how to define the scope and responsibilities of your customer education team, including where to place your team to get the most value and how to choose the portfolio of education programs that will drive behavioral change across the customer lifecycle.

2 | Customer Education as a Catalyst for Business Growth

Effective customer education requires us to have a learning strategy and to overlay that strategy across the entire customer journey. As such, it is much more than an activity that's shared across many different teams, but rather, a strategic function for the business that is accountable for achieving specific goals in the same way as other functions, like sales, marketing, and customer success.

The Importance of a Centralized Strategy for Customer Education

When you don't have a centralized holistic function that is thinking about the entire learning journey, you can't help but end up with a disjointed and fragmented experience. If your learning isn't mapped out cohesively, the customer is not nurtured from one stage to the next, and customer education becomes limited to individual projects like creating some help articles for the support team or creating an onboarding workshop with customer success. You'll end up with different teams teaching your customers different things in different ways, and customers will almost certainly experience friction as a result.

In contrast, when customer education is a strategic function, you can focus on the holistic learning journey – by dedicating a team of professionals with expertise around facilitating behavioral change through learning.

What Else Is Customer Education? And What Isn't It?

When you're creating this centralized strategic function, some fundamental principles can help you stay focused and inform what customer education is and, perhaps even more importantly, what it is not.

It Is . . . a Learning Journey That Is Overlaid on Top of the Whole Customer Journey.   That means it's not just a slice of that journey, where you end up hyperfocused on one segment like onboarding. However important a single segment is, it is never where learning definitively starts or stops.

It Is . . . Programmatic and Active.   When you create customer education, you're intentional about facilitating learning in a specific way to get specific outcomes. You have a clear program that you put in place, and the content will be contextual, depending on what stage the learners are at and who they are. It's not a passive experience, where you create a bunch of content and then wait for the customer to engage.

It Is . . . Grounded in Data.   Customer education is a constantly living and adapting entity. It is not a static artifact that becomes stale and irrelevant, but rather, it involves a continuous cycle of knowing where customers are struggling, understanding your audience, and recognizing what they need at the right time and place. It's not shooting at the hip; it is data-driven and focused to align with the learning needs of the customer.

It Is Not . . . Just about Using the Product.   The vast majority of people don't have a job that's about using your product. They have a job where your product is a tool that they can use to better complete their tasks. As a result, customer education is about helping your customers achieve success in their roles, doing the job that they hired your product to do. We'll talk more about this idea later, but the main thing to understand is that customer education thinks beyond the product. It's not about focusing on where to click but about equipping the customer with skills that allow them to thrive in their roles.

It Is Not . . . Customized 1:1 Training.   At its core, customer education is a strategy for scale. That means it's not focused on what might be effective for a single customer, but rather, it's about creating and delivering content to many different customers at the right time and at the right place. Customer education is about personalizing content so that it feels uniquely relevant to a customer's learning needs, without having to customize it.

It Is Not . . . Mandatory.   Usually, no one will be forcing your customers to engage with customer education. It's not compliance training or internal employee education. That means you need to engage and persuade your users to keep going – you need their buy-in. For this reason, customer education can't be dry and technical, and it often uses a mix of marketing elements to help the content to sing to the customer and encourage them to want to learn.

Where Should Customer Education Sit in the Business?

If we accept that the customer is always learning, from the moment they start looking for a solution to a problem all the way through to when they love your product and are telling their friends about you, then customer education has to work closely with many different business functions. The most common are marketing, product, professional services, and customer success. For this reason, it's not always easy to know where to place customer education as a business function. It doesn't have a clear and obvious home. A lot of companies house it under customer success, emphasizing the role that customer education plays in finding and maximizing value when customers need help or when you want to quicken their time to value so that they renew their subscriptions or relationship.

Other companies will place it in marketing. This works particularly well if your education plays a pivotal role in converting free tier or trial plan customers into paying customers or in attracting Educated Qualified Leads (EQLs). As customer education teams have a deep understanding and empathy for how customers are using the product, they think deeply about the industry and its needs. They have a strong understanding of both your product and the market itself. This makes customer education professionals an exceptionally good choice for creating thought leadership content to bolster the authority of your brand in your market category.

Occasionally, you'll find that customer education shows up in product teams as a way to deepen product adoption and to formalize a connection between the product and the customer base. Placing customer education here can create a connective tissue between the product itself and the customer. If your product is very complex, this can make a lot of sense. Lastly, more commonly in larger organizations, we've seen customer education crop up as a function under professional services, where training and education play a big role in driving revenue for the business.

That's Where It's Traditionally Placed. But, Where Should It Be?

All of those departments are where you might find customer education. However, while they each have benefits, placing customer education under a different department often limits the scope of what it can achieve in a way that serves the overarching goals of that function. That's why at Thought Industries, we have a Learning Strategies department with a VP who reports directly to the CEO and shares a seat at the table with the leadership team. Our charter is "Educate the market, educate the customer, and educate the team." We'll talk more about how Learning Strategies works as a department and how it can support the rest of the business in Step 7 (Chapter 9).

No matter where it sits, customer education as a strategic function is a force multiplier. It amplifies your ability to do more with less. It's a catalyst for accelerating growth throughout the customer journey. All the decisions that your customers make, from buying and adopting to renewing or expanding usage, are grounded in education. They are all about what the customer learns, and how these lessons shape their attitude and behavior.

As a scale agent for the company, it doesn't make sense to wait until you're throwing headcount at your support team or your customer onboarding process before you look to hire a customer education team. Start with the customer education function, and your business can grow proactively, ready for economies of scale.

The Customer Education Portfolio

You've got your strategic function in place, and you're ready to support the business, but what areas fall under your responsibility? Here are some of the most common programs that customer education will take ownership of, and the technology stack and expertise you'll need to run them effectively.

Knowledge Base

Also known as a help center, the knowledge base is often the first education program to come online in the lifecycle of the business. It's essentially a collection of articles that helps customers troubleshoot and find answers to their questions. Think of it like a digital instructional manual: great for self-serve and usually easy to search and filter. It is a customer education tool rather than customer education in and of itself.

Your knowledge base is a foundational program for your customer education portfolio, but it's not usually where deep learning takes place. Instead, it's more about information and knowledge transfer, and it's particularly helpful for customers who are just getting started, or who need a little help figuring out how to use a specific feature.

How to Build and Staff Your Knowledge Base   You'll likely want to explore implementing a content management system (CMS) to manage your knowledge base. Some people may choose to use a learning management system (LMS), which can help with templates for support articles, but this isn't essential. Some help centers use a GitHub repository to publish content on the website. However, if your product is complex, this can be difficult to update and maintain, and you can end up having issues with version control and management across teams or stakeholders.

In terms of staffing, start with a technical writer – preferably one who has a dash of marketing under their belt. This is because your articles need to be both digestible and concise, but also weave in the value proposition and industry best practices. If you can achieve this, then you're not only deflecting support tickets, you're also starting to explain to your customers and prospects what they can gain from using your product.

One last tip: Don't put your knowledge base behind a sign-in wall for your customers only. I'm often amazed at how often help center content is read by prospects and even people who haven't ever heard of your brand, but who have been channeled to some content during a random Google search. This is a great way to get EQLs and promote brand awareness.

Academy

This is where you'll focus much of your efforts around learning. Customer academies can also be called universities or learning centers. They usually offer courses, videos, and activities that help customers onboard and quickly find value with your products. They do this in a way that's less about knowledge transference and more about deep learning that ultimately leads to behavioral change. Content could be self-paced, eLearning content, or tutorial videos – and sometimes you'll find blended training or virtual instructor-led training (VILT). Often, your academy will start with onboarding content to help your customer find value as quickly as possible. Later, you can supplement onboarding content with deeper or broader learning tracks that help your customers develop mastery with your products. You can even create a certification to demonstrate this proficiency. Eventually, you can expand your content strategy to continuing education, helping customers become experts – not only with your product, but also in their industry. For example, at Thought Industries, it isn't enough that we teach you how to use our platform. We also want to teach you how to create exceptional learning experiences so that the product becomes a canvas for your own customer education strategy.

How to Build and Staff Your Academy   You'll definitely want an LMS to create and manage your academy – preferably one that specializes in customer learning. A lot of people make the mistake of only thinking about what they need right now, but you should look for one that scales with your program beyond your first year. It's a huge pain to rip out an LMS and replace it. Look for an LMS with customization options and ways to personalize content that's aligned with the different audiences in your customer base. As we said earlier, you need your customers to want to be here, so engagement and consumption-driving features are a must-have. Make sure that your LMS offers deep integration with other business tools, like ecommerce functionality so that you can charge for the content you're producing, the videoconferencing software you're using for VILT (such as Zoom), the CMS that you're using for your knowledge base, your customer relationship management (CRM) such as Salesforce, and your support ticket software. Don't settle for anything less than advanced reporting capabilities that provide a true understanding of the impact of your learning on the business. For the content that lives on your LMS, you'll find it a lot easier if you have native authoring tools available, but you can supplement these with video and audio editing software such as Camtasia and potential eLearning authoring software like Articulate or Captivate.

When you're thinking about how to staff your academy, look to hire instructional designers, sometimes called learning experience designers. These will be people who can create learning experiences optimized for learning transference. You may also want an academy program manager to holistically stay on top of the academy's progress and look for ways to expand and collaborate across the organization. As it's a different skillset, you might want to hire an LMS administrator who can handle the back-end technical configuration of the LMS itself. The content you want to include in your academy may also dictate what staff you need – for example, trainers for instructor-led training (ILT) or someone with experience in psychometrics for building exams or certifications.

In-Product Education

Next up in the customer education portfolio is in-product education (IPE). One of the most effective ways you can teach your customer is in context of the task they're performing. Rather than ask a customer to leave your product to learn about something, why not teach them just in time, when they're actually using it? Conventionally, IPE is focused on performance support, guiding customers to perform a specific task. This is more akin to a knowledge base program rather than deep learning and encouraging longer, more sustainable behavioral change.

However, more and more companies are discovering the impact of offering deeper learning experiences within the product, such as videos and interactive quizzes or activities. In fact, in many cases we've started to see the idea of an academy and IPE slowly converging, where fully fledged academies are popping up from within the product itself, and customers can access all the learning in-product.

How to Build and Staff Your In-Product Education   It's vital to build and staff your IPE. You'll want a digital adoption platform (DAP) like WalkMe or Pendo. You can build your own IPE, or you can use a tool like Thought Industries that surfaces content from within your product. While your instructional designers can support creating these experiences, you'll want to make sure that someone on your team works closely with the product to create super-engaging, concise learning experiences that fit the bill.

Community

Sometimes marketing owns customer online communities, but we think it fits nicely within customer education's remit, because the primary function of a customer community is to connect and learn from one another. A *community* is a channel for experts and advocates to influence and teach one another. An active customer community is a powerful support ticket deflection tool. You can use your community to ask questions, get feedback, and even draw threads to create new content.

How to Build and Staff Your Community   Community platform software like Insided will make it really easy to create, manage, and moderate your community. You can't get away without a dedicated community manager; they are essential because they moderate, encourage, promote, reach out, and manage the overall experience. Without one, you're seriously hampering the community's growth, and it's likely to fail.

Sometimes you'll find that communities pop up where people are naturally interacting, like on LinkedIn, Facebook, or Reddit. It's important to have someone with social media skills who can merge ideas together and follow and participate in communities wherever they might be. As a general rule, organic social media communities lack the sophistication, moderation, and customization to form a dedicated customer community that achieves brand advocacy or community-driven content. For this, you'll want a separate, clearly defined experience.

Blog, Social Media, and Email

You'll usually find the blog, email marketing, and social media accounts housed under marketing, but customer education is beginning to take on some of these responsibilities, too. This is especially true if your customer education program functions as a center of excellence focused on the industry to which your customers belong. Blogs and social media are a great way to address the learning needs of potential customers earlier in the funnel, but they're super helpful for your customers, too! It's unrealistic in the modern era to assume that people are always going to head to your academy and learn. It's much more likely that they will find something by Googling organically, while they're scrolling through a social media feed, or because of a well-timed email marketing campaign. People are learning everywhere, from YouTube to TikTok, and you need a strategy in place for that. Customer education has a perspective around the industry that other departments may not have; we understand what people need to learn, and we have plenty of experience developing engaging content. If this content isn't under your purview, make sure you're at least a close contributor with the content marketing team.

How to Build and Staff Your Blog and Social Media Accounts   If you're taking the wheel with marketing content like the company blog and social media accounts, your technology stack is actually catchy videos and snappy content! What you really need here is just a content strategist who is savvy around social media and knows how to create engagement levels that go through the roof.

Fee Versus Free: Should You Monetize Your Customer Education Content?

The final decision to make at this stage is whether your customer education program will be a cost center, a cost-recovery center, or a profit center for the business. In a cost-center model, you're spending more money than you're making; a cost-recovery center will aim to break even; and a profit center earns direct revenues. As your customer education program matures, you will probably find yourself wondering how to move from being a cost center that helps other teams scale to being a revenue-generating arm of the business in its own right.

Remember That Training Has Value

In a 2021 webinar with Thought Industries, Maria Manning-Chapman from TSIA spoke about how, if your customer education department remains a cost-center, you'll always be similar to the teenager going to their parents for money when they want to go out with their friends.[1] In short, if you're not making your own money, you don't have control over your own behavior or growth.

We know many customer education professionals who are reluctant to charge for customer education, often citing that they don't want a price tag to be a "barrier" to learning content consumption. However, the barrier to content consumption is more often related to a lack of consumption strategies than it is to whether training content has been monetized. There are many programs that have customers who gladly pay for valuable training content! In fact, benchmark data suggests that the split between fee-based and free content is about 75 percent paid to 25 percent free. Sure, no one is going to start charging for support articles or marketing content – that's included as part of the 25 percent. However, when you think about that 75 percent, whether it's going to help the customer get better at their job, provide a certification for their resume, give them some kind of digital badge

---

[1] Maria Manning-Chapman, "Fee and Free, Strategies and Considerations for Monetizing Customer Training," Webinar, August 2021, https://www.tsia.com/webinars/free-and-fee-strategies-and-considerations-for-monetizing-customer-training.

for their LinkedIn, or open their eyes to industry best practices – that's worth a price tag.

Don't be worried that charging for content will turn the customer off from engaging. When people pay for content, they are often intrinsically more motivated to see training through than they would be if the content was provided for free. The cost of the education is a signal to the market that says, "Hey! This training has value, it's going to help you in your career – it's worth your time." Most users are comfortable with the idea that these benefits come with a price tag and may even see the training as more desirable because of the cost.

Land and Expand

A smart monetization strategy will help you decide what content should be part of your free 25 percent and what should go in the other 75 percent. You may want to offer free training at the start of the customer journey – for example, in the form of webinars, user guides, or even a digital learning platform. As your users move through their lifecycle with you, you can then offer paid opportunities like eLearning, instructor-led training, or larger-scale certifications. You might create "premium" content focused on specific use cases or domain expertise. Many customers would gladly pay for training that is tailored to the specific way they want to use your product. Map out an ideal customer journey that takes your users through both free and paid content, and think about the ratio that works for you.

The formative decisions around scope and strategy that we've discussed in this chapter are essential points to consider, and will be the foundation of your customer education, playing a large role in proving your value overall. Now, with that in mind, let's turn to the 12 steps of the *Customer Education Playbook* itself and see how you can develop a clear and structured approach that leads to impactful, engaging, and measurable programs. Let's dive in!

3

Step 1: Maximize Impact by Aligning Customer Education to Business Goals

Customer education is a challenge, and the stakes are high. Without identifying your goals from the outset, you risk executing aimlessly, and you'll struggle to help others understand the impact of your work.

So, consider this: What do you want to get out of your customer education program?

This question is less about your customer education team itself and more about looking to the rest of the organization for guidance. Customer education teams don't work in a silo; they interact with many different functions of the business to help solve a wide range of challenges. To achieve success, the goals of customer education need to align with the overarching objectives of the company. In fact, the success of your customer education program hinges on executive support and buy-in, which can only happen if you make sure that you share a vision. If your goals aren't aligned, you'll end up doing a lot of work that isn't relevant for what the business is doing right now, and you're not going to get the executive support that you need to keep scaling and growing your program.

Five Common Business Goals for Customer Education

In this chapter, we'll cover five common business objectives and how you can align your own customer education goals to them to achieve success. For each example, we'll also identify the metrics you can use to measure your program and tangibly prove to the C-suite that the customer education program has a clear return on investment (ROI) in areas like generating direct revenue, reducing existing costs, or attracting new leads.

Goal 1: Improve Product Adoption

Product adoption challenges can come in many forms. Perhaps your business is releasing new features and customers aren't using them. Or maybe you have an onboarding issue, where customers who are new to your product are feeling overwhelmed or they aren't getting value during those critical first 90 days. It could even be that customers aren't adopting your product at all.

If product adoption is an organizational focus in your business, then your customer education program needs to ask, "How can customer education help to drive product adoption and fix the problem we're facing right now?" For example, if customers aren't adopting the product in the first place, you might want to create a prescriptive learning path for new customers that walks them through getting started. If the issue is that customers aren't trying out new features, you could launch content targeted specifically around those features. At Thought Industries, we create Feature Spotlight videos that focus on a single feature and the value it can provide to the user. As a direct result, I've seen huge growth in the adoption of empty state features, which previously had zero uptake before the content was created and released.

Of course, in some situations, adoption will be mandatory, such as a retail franchise that is onboarding a new point-of-sale product, such as a cash register. In this example, a product adoption challenge could be that users are making mistakes when they are first onboarded onto the solution – they're just not adopting it in the right way. A similar solution in this case would be to create a walkthrough or a tutorial for the first interaction for each new employee handling the machine to reduce or eliminate error.

Don't Talk about the Product!

It may seem counterintuitive, but an essential part of using customer education to boost product adoption is to remember that your customers and prospects don't care about your product! One of the most famous and often-quoted adages in marketing was coined by Theodore Levitt, who said, "People don't want to buy a quarter-inch drill, they want a quarter-inch hole.[1] It's outcomes that matter, not the product that facilitates that outcome.

Let's look at an example using a landing page builder app. If your training focuses on how to use the features of creating a landing page, such as how to enter a heading or add links, it doesn't deal with what users are really looking for. Rather than thinking about what the product does, think about the principles of landing page conversion and optimization. Your users want to generate sales, not just build a landing page. Education that focuses on how to build a page that's optimized for conversion, SEO, or best-practice design will be far more impactful.

Bottom line? Look to create customer education that talks about use cases and puts the value proposition as the star of the show rather than focus entirely on features and functionality. Your customers have hired your product to do a specific job, and what they really want to know is how it's going to help them make their lives easier.

---

[1] Clayton M. Christensen, *The Clayton M. Christensen Reader* (Harvard Business Review Press, 2016), 46.

Made to Measure: How to Prove ROI for Product Adoption

If you're a large enterprise, you may have the traffic and infrastructure available to you to distribute various types of content and test out different scenarios. For example, you might randomly distribute your customers into two groups and then run an experiment where one group watches a "Getting Started" video and the other does not. Then, you could track consumption rates and adoption rates over the first 30 days and get meaningful information on a causal relationship between your content and user behavior.

However, in the vast majority of cases, this probably isn't realistic. Instead, here are two other ways you can measure the success of your content on product adoption.

Trained/Not Trained Cohort Analysis   In this analysis, you simply compare the behavior of two different groups: one trained, one not. First, you'll need to define *trained*. To do this, create content that users need to opt into, like video content that you have to register for and watch, a guidebook that needs to be downloaded, or anything else you can actually track. You'll then compare the people who interacted with the content ("trained") to those who didn't ("not trained") and measure product adoption rates between the two groups. Although this isn't a causal analysis, it'll still give you a great understanding of the relationship between consuming that content and product adoption rates.

Pre/Post Content Cohort Analysis   With this approach, you push the customer education content to all of your customers by, for example, creating a three-minute video that new users watch the first time they sign into your product environment. You then track the data for product adoption after this content has been viewed, measuring the difference between the metrics you had before you launched the video. If you can get the support of your business leaders to push content to all of your users, this can be a great replacement for a true A/B experiment. While the pre/post analysis is also correlative and not causal, it more or less controls for confounding variables.

Goal 2: Scale Customer Support

Reducing the impact on the support team is a common business goal, and for good reason. As your company grows, it's natural that the number of tickets you get is going to scale with it, and no, unfortunately it doesn't matter *how* intuitive and easy your product is to use. What are you going to do to meet this need? Are you going to keep hiring more support agents, indefinitely? Obviously, that doesn't scale. Instead, you must figure out how you can deflect support tickets, and the best way to do that is through customer education.

Scaling your support offerings through customer education comes in the form of self-service resources. Whether that's help centers, online communities, or FAQs, self-service customer education can have a big impact on scaling your support team through documentation and resources.

Let's look in detail at one of these examples – online communities. These are often thought of as a means to build brand enthusiasm and customer advocacy. However, when done right, they can also play a huge role in ticket deflection. Customers can turn to the community with pressing questions, and an active community can often generate answers more quickly than a support team. On top of this, the best communities include experts with knowledge, experience, and best practices that can outweigh your in-house experience 10 to 1.

Of course, a successful community doesn't spring up overnight. You can't just build an online forum and expect it to succeed. This isn't *Field of Dreams*. Most communities suffer from the tumbleweed effect. The chemistry of a thriving online community takes a lot of work to spark it into lift and requires investment to nurture it from the ground up, from attracting new members to moderating conversations and helping it to scale and grow.

Stop Thinking about Self-Serve as a Compromise

Once upon a time, self-service meant doing something yourself to save on money or time, often at the expense of the experience. Think about it. A self-service café, even at its best, cannot match the experience delivered by a fine-dining restaurant. Mowing your own lawn might not get you those smooth lines, but hey – you've saved a few dollars in the process.

With the rise of digital experiences, however, this is no longer the case. Self-service is now synonymous with speed, agility, flexibility, and satisfaction. Customers don't have to sit on hold or wait for an agent to get back to them via email. When it comes to customer education, you can use self-service to empower your users to get more out of your product.

Of course, that doesn't mean your support reps can't get the ball rolling. With the right content and training in hand, support interactions can be transformed into learning experiences, and as your support agents continue fielding tickets, they can begin to create macros in response to the specific kinds of questions that they're being asked. The macros could include links to helpful resources, a recommendation for additional training content, or even the support agent themselves doing a quick tutorial on the spot. In this way, your customer education program begins to transform support interactions into learning experiences and even operationalizes them in the moment.

Made to Measure: How to Show the Success in Scaling Customer Support

Your main metric for this goal is ticket deflection rate. Your support tickets will naturally scale with the growth of your customer base. However, once you invest in self-service resources, you will see that trend reverse. With each additional month, more self-service resources become available, and more customers join your community to offer one another help and support. Customers will file fewer support tickets even as your company expands.

Figure 3.1 shows how the customer education team at Optimizely presented the relationship between self-service and ticket deflection. The day we launched Optiverse (a self-service resource hub for Optimizely customers), support tickets plummeted, even while the number of customers continued to grow.

You can do this kind of visual representation for individual support ticket categories, too, and clearly illustrate how customer education can solve a specific issue. Look at the challenges that attract the greatest

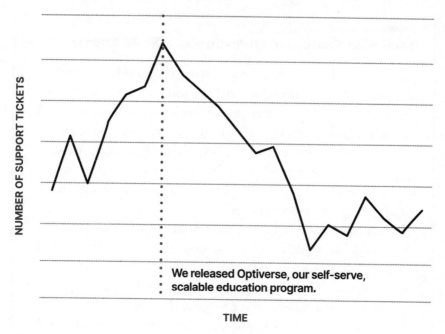

Figure 3.1 Optimizely Support Ticket Deflection

number of tickets in your organization and create targeted content that allows users to self-serve that problem. This could be anything from "How do I change my account info?" to "How do I turn off that cat filter on Zoom?" Present a time-based line graph that shows ticket requests for this issue over time, with a clear callout for when you launch the support materials.

Goal 3: Maximize Customer Success

Every time a new customer is onboarded to your product, your customer success managers (CSMs) have the same conversation. They may have these conversations dozens of times a week; they could probably recite them word-for-word in their sleep. Does this sound like your company? If so, then your CSMs are massively underleveraged. How can they offer deep strategic value if they're always dealing with basics?

Daniel on Customer Education as a Scale Engine

When I led customer education at Asana, I reported into customer success, and I was dismayed to learn on my first day that my director – who I liked and respected – was leaving. We took a walk and I asked him about his thoughts on the role of customer education. He explained that he had a lightbulb moment when he realized that he had been traditionally building customer success teams by starting with CSMs first and foremost, so that as the organization grew, accounts could get the value and training that they needed. However, he had since realized that to keep up with the growth, he would need to hire more and more CSMs. Instead, he had recognized that it made a lot more sense to start with a customer education program, and then the whole customer success team would be in a better place to scale. He could ensure the team had on-demand training in place, and he would need fewer CSMs to do repeat training. This mirrors the idea we spoke about back in Chapter 2, that customer education is a scale engine that allows you to build your organization far more proactively.

If your customer education team is tasked with maximizing customer success, try asking your CSMs to list the things that they say repeatedly to most of their customers: the standard onboarding questions that they answer, the company information they provide, or even the sales pitch repeated for new customers who join the account. If you can create content that covers this material, then you're leaving your CSMs with a lot more time to deal with more nuanced questions around use cases, which is likely to offer far more strategic value to your customers.

One idea to cover this material is to run an ongoing live webinar program teaching the basics of your product, and then strongly promote it to new customers. If your product is relatively complex, you might also run additional webinars to teach more advanced material. You can also record on-demand versions of the webinar. Then, you can provide these prerecorded versions to customers whenever they choose, or you can schedule to play them live at a regular cadence, while ensuring someone is standing by for live questions.

Is It Working? How to Assess Learning Experiences

It's one thing to offer learning; it's another to know whether learning takes place. It's not enough to set up a learning experience; you must also ensure that you know whether your material is making a difference.

One practical way to see when customers are ready for the next level of strategic conversations with CSMs is to create a commonly accepted signal that shows that customers have a certain level of foundational knowledge. On a basic or initial level, this signal could be based on such metrics as percentage of training starts or completes, drop-off points, or the amount of time spent training. For a signal that you can use for a more advanced user, you can also set up a credential or an award that's based on passing a well-designed assessment. Sometimes described as *getting certified*, passing the test would result in a credential of some kind: a certificate or even a digital badge to post on LinkedIn.

At Optimizely, in an effort to increase customer value, the customer success team implemented a "Get Trained" program that prompted customers to get product certified by a certain date and gently nudged them toward this goal. In an initial kick-off call, the CSM would outline the training program and would mention that they would speak again once the training was complete. It was up to customers to decide how they wanted to learn the product. They could choose between courses, webinars, YouTube videos, and more, as long as they could pass the test. Customers would be prompted to complete the training, and on completion, the CSMs would get a notification to book the next strategy meeting, where they could congratulate the customer on completing the training and see what the customer needed next. While previously CSMs had felt that they were constantly dealing with very basic questions, after this program was put into place, CSMs spent far more time providing strategic value, and they reported that customers were asking much more sophisticated questions.

Made to Measure: Proving the Quantitative Worth of Supporting CSMs

In your efforts to scale customer success, you'll want to focus on improving several metrics. First, ensure that your customers are actually engaging with your education by tracking and improving the percentage of customer accounts who have completed the content. If your product touches multiple users, measure depth as well as breadth. That is, in addition to getting more accounts trained, you'll also want to get more users on each account trained.

Second, create a source of explicit data by asking your CSMs the same question periodically. Something like, "On a scale of 1–10, how strategic have your conversations with customers been?" Then, augment that with qualitative data: Interview your CSMs to get a sense of how the education has helped them in their roles.

Third, check to see whether your education impacted customers further down the funnel. What does lifetime value (LTV) look like for trained customers versus untrained customers? What does *churn* (turnover) look like? In other words, measure the impact of customer education in the same way you measure the impact of customer success.

Finally, one of the best ways to determine whether you're scaling customer success requires you to track how customer education impacts time to value (TTV) – the amount of time it takes for new customers to realize value from your product. A goal of customer education is to reduce TTV so that your customers are gaining value as quickly as possible, with minimal friction.

If your company is not currently tracking TTV, we highly recommend you start. To do so, you must first define what *value* means. More specifically, what does value mean to your customers? What is their "*aha!*" moment? And how is that value "captured" as a metric (or cluster of metrics) in your product? In the next chapter, you'll learn more about how to define success for your customers and strategically improve their perceived value.

Goal 4: Create Brand Ambassadors

If your organization's goals are about building advocates, product champions, or brand ambassadors, then your customer education should work to build better brand trust and loyalty. What you want are customers who will spread the word about your product and tell their friends about you. To do so, they need to be totally bought into the value of your product or service, which not only means you need to move people from being novices to masters, but also to seeing your product as indispensable.

To create learning experiences that build advocacy, look to craft a learning journey that encourages three things:

1. Mastery
2. Delight
3. Connection

These ingredients make up the secret sauce of brand advocacy. For example, you might offer the opportunity to complete a course (mastery) that earns you a digital badge (delight), which you can then post and share on social media or in a customer forum (connection). Throughout this education path, you can also encourage your users to make their everyday work easier using your product, which can help them see you as an indispensable tool.

Once you've developed mastery, delight, and connection, you need to provide avenues for your brand ambassadors to advocate on your behalf. Think about creating community moderators in your forums, for example, or asking for guest experts to join your webinars and post thought leadership content on your website. Provide direct opportunities for your customers to promote you, such as via referrals, regional in-person meet-ups of advocates and prospects, or train-the-trainer programs, where your advocates are channeling that delight to work on your behalf.

Engage the Social Side

Social learning has been shown to exponentially magnify loyalty and enthusiasm in your customers. Look for ways to give existing advocates an everyday opportunity to share their best practices and network with peers, and make sure they have an audience to listen to them rave about you! These everyday avenues can be customer forums, social media channels, or even in-person events. According to Forrester's Benchmark B2B Social Marketing Efforts report, 75 percent of customers who utilized community-generated information have greater satisfaction on using your product, which of course leads to better brand loyalty.

Made to Measure: How to Track Brand Ambassadors

Start with your easy metrics. If you have a certification program, how many customers are getting certified or expressing interest in certification? How many members have you added to your online community, if relevant? These numbers show how well you're doing in reaching and engaging your audience. You'll also want to measure the impact of these programs by comparing the behaviors of two cohorts: those who are engaging with your content and those who are not.

One critical business metric that you should be using to validate the impact of your program on brand advocacy is the net promoter score (NPS). For example, ask, "What is the average NPS of customers who are engaged with the online community versus customers who are not?" NPS is based on a single question your users answer: "On a scale of 0–10, how likely are you to recommend our business to a friend or colleague?" Looking back at Asana, there was a strong correlation between NPS and course completion: customers who completed Asana Academy courses were far more likely to recommend Asana to friends and colleagues!

You can also look at customer lifetime value (LTV) to see if it improves as users consume your training content. Generally speaking, we've noticed that as users become more mature and sophisticated with your product, they unlock its full potential, which in turn will often lead them to become advocates of your brand. Training speeds up the process.

If you have more resources at your disposal, you can create a maturity model for your product or service, and then define a path to measure the impact of your education on LTV. Start by defining the behaviors or the cluster of behaviors that customers do at different stages of maturity with your product. For Asana novices, it might have been to sign in and create a task. For Twitter, it might be sending your first Tweet or following 10 people. At Caterpillar, it might be driving a tractor.

At the other end of the spectrum are much more mature behaviors. At Asana, it might be creating a portfolio with a certain number of projects inside and inviting a dozen collaborators. At Twitter it could be creating lists, scheduling tweets, having 100,000 followers, or tweeting five times each day. At Caterpillar, it might be performing complex maneuvers with an excavator. Once you decide how to differentiate a novice from a master, you can then follow the relationship between their level of expertise and how deeply they've engaged with your educational content.

Goal 5: Lead Your Market Category

If your organization's main goal is to generate demand by becoming an established thought or industry leader, that's an important goal to get aligned with. Often, creating this kind of content will come from taking a step back from the product to talk to your customers about what they need to understand to do their jobs better. If you have a cybersecurity product, for example, it's great to teach your users how to set up policies and rules using the software, but it's more impactful to help them gain buy-in on a cyber-security policy, give advice on how to protect and secure remote teams, or how to "shift left" to make developers' lives easier. If you can help them overcome these real challenges that they face day-to-day, you're well on your way to being a thought or industry leader.

If you do thought leadership right, you're publishing agnostic infor-mation that's focused on the job rather than the tool. Your users will begin to associate their job with your product, creating strong associations between the two (similar to how HubSpot is synonymous with inbound marketing). As a result, when users buy your product, they also feel that they're getting both product and also *industry* expertise; that is, your cus-tomers will believe they're gaining a partner who can help them achieve success in their job.

Make Marketing Your New Best Friend

"Hey, that's marketing's job, not ours!"

Sure, you might well have a whole marketing team focused on creating top-of-the-funnel thought leadership content, and that's great. Our advice to you is, get involved! Look at your team as learning experience design-ers. You are a group of subject matter experts in the industry, and you have a lot to offer thought leadership. You might even be the best team to *drive* thought leadership by creating actionable resources that help marketing to do their job.

Being effective is not about separating out which role belongs to whom; it's about making sure that education is part of the larger business conversation, wherever it happens.

Made to Measure: How Can You Track Your Market Leadership?

As we've said before, start with the low-hanging fruit. The easy metrics, like webinar registrations and e-book downloads, can show growth. Once you have those in place, look further afield to search results or organic search hits, items that show people are thinking about your brand. Take a look at your social media activity: not only followers, but also mentions and interactions, and track what content leads to a boost in numbers. Over time, you can also track more big-ticket items, like speaking engagements, analyst mentions, awards, or mentions in industry publications and review sites.

Adam Avramescu is a leader in the customer education field and author of *Customer Education: How Smart Companies Profit by Making Customers Smarter*. Below, he reflects on how he has defined the goals of customer education in programs he has led.

Thoughts from . . . Adam Avramescu, Customer Education Leader and Host of CELab Podcast

If I think back, the goals for customer education have been different at every organization in which I've worked, and that's influenced how I've built each program. Typically, when I first come into an organization, there may not be explicit goals laid out, but there is usually some kind of initial need; something going on in their business that makes the company want to invest in customer education. The first thing I do, even when I'm interviewing for the role, is figure out what stage the company is at, and ask questions about what they are trying to achieve. What's the customer's "job to be done" and what are the pain points that are stopping them from achieving that? Where do the product's capabilities intersect with that customer goal?

I also ask about wider business goals. What growth targets is the company trying to achieve? What product-market fit do they have? Internally, what is the company currently doing ad hoc or reactively that they could be doing in a more defined or organized way? I build out my goals for customer education from there.

For example, when I started at Optimizely, a company deeply focused on experimentation and digital optimization, customer education was a new concept for the company, but the rationale for investing in customer education was to help our CSMs and support agents become more effective, and to scale the work they were doing one-on-one with clients. They had a lot of support reps who were working inefficiently, re-creating the wheel time and time again. Our early customers, who had used A/B testing and optimization products before, knew fairly intuitively how to use our product. But as we grew, customers who hadn't used a product like ours needed a lot of hand-holding to get to meaningful use of the product. Because our CSMs couldn't scale support, a lot of customers weren't getting to that meaningful value. They didn't know how to structure meaningful A/B tests, or how to interpret the results of the ones they did run. It's not surprising that this resulted in a lot of churn. This wasn't unique to Optimizely; I commonly see companies decide to start a customer education program with a goal to reduce the manual or repetitive effort for CSMs delivering training and support.

I've found that executive goals are likely to be more strategic rather than process-based, and it's important to get a sense of that, too. I like to ask about this when I first meet executives: What are your company-level goals? What initiatives does the company want to drive? At Optimizely, when I joined, we were fighting what they called a "war on Gold churn," trying to retain self-serve "Gold Plan" customers paying $499 a month, who were churning because they failed to get value from our product. It was important to help these customers be successful, but deeply unprofitable to provide dedicated support and account management to each of them. Revisiting

(continued)

company-level goals over time is important: as Optimizely grew and moved upmarket, our goals and priorities changed. Years in, retaining self-service customers was no longer as high on the list of business priorities, and so our customer education goals needed to evolve to suit.

In retrospect, I probably should have asked more of these kinds of questions in my early days at Optimizely. When my leaders set out priorities for me and my team, they often asked for it in terms of tangible content like creating a webinar series or fixing a knowledge base, and with a background in instructional design it was easy for me to focus on content and learner experience without explicitly thinking about aligning with the company goals. I could have saved a lot of time and made fewer mistakes if I'd had the mindset I have now, and had looked for that bigger business problem.

At Checkr, where I worked after Optimizely, it was a very different story. I was more mature as a customer education leader, so I knew what questions to ask. But the actual product – background check software – was different, and the motivations for customer education were new for me. While background checks are usually seen as a way to "keep people out" of jobs, Checkr has a mission to "build a better future by making hiring fairer." As a result, a large part of my role was to educate clients on how to evaluate their candidates more fairly, and to balance their trust and safety goals with their compliance obligations. This, again, is an example of how your education program should highlight the intersection where the product meets a real customer need.

At Slack – different company, different product, different goals once again – they already had millions of users when I started. They had a successful self-serve business, great documentation, and they already had Slackbot delivering education. This was a much more mature customer education program than in my previous start-ups, but deploying a product like Slack across a large enterprise organization requires different approaches to learning and change management. Our opportunity was to build enterprise-ready education that would serve our largest customers. Compared to previous customer education programs I've led, my team at Slack builds and delivers deeper services that are more prescriptive, but for a smaller handful of accounts. This leads us to measure things like our customers' certification rates, and how we drive deeper adoption and maturity across our enterprise clients.

Think Strategically

One piece of advice I'd give on setting goals for customer education is to think strategically. I remember a point at Optimizely where my boss at the time felt our team wasn't meeting expectations. They said that we weren't moving fast enough or solving customer problems. I needed to find and achieve quicker wins that would prove value, and then get more proactive about solving larger customer needs and aligning those with business metrics. This was a turning point for me. I realized that if executives were going to trust me, and care about customer education, they needed to see me doing more than churning out content; they needed to understand the story of what I was doing.

We had launched a webinar series that just hadn't moved the needle on customer retention, and in hindsight, I can see that we didn't know why customers were churning in the first place, so a webinar on how to use the product wasn't going to help! We changed tack and started doing more strategic work to improve the knowledge base, fill gaps in search terms, and target areas where we knew CS were answering the same questions over and over. We analyzed the largest ticket categories and used customer feedback to decide what content to create, improve, or deprecate . . . and we started hitting the mark more consistently.

As a result, CS had more time to focus on deeper problems, and we could use data on ticket deflection rates and onboarding

(continued)

efficiency to prove our impact. This gave us leverage to move onto other projects across the business. For example, customers were telling the CSMs that they needed help to go from 0–60 faster, and after several iterations, that became the basis of Optiverse, our consolidated support community, academy, and resource center. The product team was running in-product education and onboarding guides, but they realized it made sense for us to take ownership and enhance those programs so we could drive better product adoption and convert more free trials to paid accounts. We had launch managers onboarding enterprise customers, but we were able to take ownership of that process too, and build a training services function. As we continued to prove value, our customer education portfolio grew, and we got more buy-in to create our own projects, too.

Measure Value

When it comes to measuring the success of education, I've found that there's a balance to strike. On the one hand, being able to prove ROI doesn't substitute for executive sponsorship. You'll often get asked, "How can we prove that customer education moves the needle with our customer?" but that type of data won't be available until you've educated enough customers to actually see the impact. Executives need to recognize that they aren't going to get access to direct data immediately, and that this will grow over time. However, you also have a responsibility to tell the story of how customer education drives growth in the business, and that's ultimately how you're going to earn trust.

So, ask yourself – what *can* you measure? Can you look at ticket deflection, discoverability, or consumption around your programs? Can you show how you're iterating your content and moving in the right direction? This could be page views, enrollments to academy tracks, satisfaction rate, or even qualitative data like customer survey answers. Over time, you'll be able to capture more value goals, such as an analysis of trained versus untrained and the impact on adoption, or the number of customers reaching time to value.

It is so critical to start your customer education program with a strong understanding of what the business's overarching goals are, and to ensure that you are ready to measure the impact of your education according to those goals. This is how you can ensure ahead of time that your success will also be a win for the company as a whole. Your next step will be to turn your thoughts to your customers – what does their success look like?

4

Step 2: Motivate Customers by Curating Their Path to Awesome

Now that you've considered what your program is looking to achieve, it's important to differentiate between your organization's goals and the goals of your customers. When you think about what success means from the customer's point of view, it's not always going to naturally align with how your business defines success. If your company has a goal to increase revenue this year, you'll have trouble finding volunteers who have made it a priority to give you their money. If your organizational objective is to increase product adoption, you'll need to give customers a reason to adopt it.

Instead of purely focusing on your company's goals, you need to motivate your customers to behave in a certain way by meeting *their* needs. The customer may not have a direct need to adopt your product, but they do have a need that adopting your product will *solve*.

This is why it's so important to define your customer's goals independently of your product. You might instinctively think that the role of customer education is to train users on how to use your product, but in reality, that's not where you should focus—at least, not entirely.

Instead, customer education must put the value proposition front and center. First, look to understand how the customer defines success, and next, how you can design learning that allows your product to fit in as a tool to help achieve that success.

How Do I Work Out What "Success" Looks Like?

Success will look different for each customer, but in the context of using your product, it's almost always related to customers performing their role with less effort and with more accuracy. In other words, customers "hire" your product to help them accomplish more than they would have otherwise. Of course, not all your customers will have the same job. That means that a good starting point is to think about who your customers are. Think broadly here, and include not just the person signing on the dotted line, but also the people who will be using the product every day or helping out behind the scenes.

For any given SaaS product, you may be dealing with a purchasing team who make the initial decision, a core department that is going to deploy the technology in the service of their jobs, and then key stakeholders from teams such as finance, IT, or even HR who need to be involved in the life-cycle of the product. They all have different roles, so the value proposition will look different for each of these customer segments. Remember, what's transformational for an administrator is not the same as what's going to speak to a conventional user.

If you have a horizontal product that cuts across industries, you may also need to think about how those needs differ from one industry to another. A marketing team's day job is different from a consulting agency, for example, so they will see value differently and need an alternate learning journey. This could be as simple as creating two customer education paths and asking users to self-select their persona when they enter your website or engage with your materials, but to make it happen, you have to identify that segment to begin with.

Once you've identified these segments and personas, do an analysis of the jobs that each customer is doing. You can then understand how they could be using your product to make that job easier or more accurate and design effective learning around that value proposition.

In practice, creating content using customer goals is the difference between saying, "Here's how to use Zoom," and saying, "Here's how to conduct effective remote meetings using Zoom." Conducting remote meetings is part of the customer's job, and you're using education to support them in making that job easier, with your product as the tool that helps them get there.

Expect That Customer Goals Will Evolve Over Time

Remember that defining customer goals is not a "set it and forget it" kind of task. You'll need to consider what customers need to learn at each step along their journey with your business. Otherwise, you might find that you're not aligning education with the right needs.

For example, assume your product is a task management software, and you have a customer who has an overall need to be more productive and efficient at work.

Early on, your business is probably thinking about how to acquire new users, and your customers are probably thinking about how to overcome their productivity gap. Later in the journey, however, when users become more advanced customers, they may not be interested in education that targets this productivity challenge anymore. They've moved on to other challenges, such as how to widen adoption of the product in the business. Though the customers haven't changed, their mastery over the product has evolved and their needs have changed. Your customer education has to change to suit their needs, or risk losing their interest.

Creating Aha! Moments

By now, you should have a pretty solid understanding of who your customers are and the everyday challenges they face in their jobs. Next on the agenda is to connect your offering to those needs. For that, you need to define your product's "aha!" moments.

An aha! moment is, at its core, an emotional, highly impactful experience for the user during which they suddenly realize that this product or service is going to help them make progress. In an aha! moment, a user can tangibly see that your product is going to make a real difference in their work. These moments are transformational in terms of brand loyalty and adoption, and so they are essential to capture and understand.

Identifying Aha! Moments

You can isolate these aha! moments using a mixture of quantitative and qualitative research. Start with your analytics, whether you manage those in-house or you integrate with a tool like Mixpanel, Heap, or Pendo. Take a look at the correlations between customers with sustained product adoption or the common behaviors in customers who renew their licenses. These are groups of customers who, by definition, see value in your product, so that data is great to leverage to determine which moments matter. At the same time, look at the converse: the customers who churn or who don't adopt your product. What actions or clusters of actions are the first group engaging in that the non-adopted customers aren't? Doing this exercise greatly helps you identify the moments that matter most to your customers.

Analytics are valuable, but we can't emphasize enough how important it is to talk to your customers, too. This qualitative research is essential, both with your sustained-use customers and the ones who churn. Ask your engaged customers, *"What do you love about the product? What value do you get from using it?"* For disengaged customers, ask, *"Why didn't you stick around? What was lacking for you?"*

As discussed above, user needs change over time. Make sure to define user expectations at the earliest stages of product adoption as well as periodically throughout the journey. You can do this using onboarding assessments, quarterly business reviews, or an automated solution like a customer survey.

If you don't currently have a stream of explicit data that lets you hear from your customers, add one! I've seen many organizations that get tied up in trying to make sense of implicit data such as search queries and content analytics such as consumption rates, when actually they could make their lives easier by just asking their customers how they feel about the product and if their goals have changed lately. In many cases, a metric such as a net promoter score (NPS) can tell you everything you need to know about whether you're providing value. Make it easier on yourself by adding that source of explicit data that you can tap into if you're asking yourself what the customer wants.

Daniel at Asana: A Case Study in Defining Success for the Customer

At Asana, we had an organizational goal to *"Make adoption drop-dead easy."* My initial thought was that customer education could easily align with that business goal. But then I took a step back and thought: Do I actually know what customers need to make it easy for them to adopt our product? How could I motivate them to adopt the product, if I didn't know what was driving their adoption behind the scenes? The answer wasn't clear.

As well as using existing quantitative data, we decided to create a new source of qualitative data that was focused on answering this question and on uncovering the motivator for our customers. We created our own initial assumptions, then sent a survey to all customers who were engaging with educational content to ask them explicit questions like:

> *What do you wish you knew at the start of your Asana journey?*
> *What would you have liked to learn first?*
> *What was the aha! moment that helped you realize you were getting value?*
> *What did you learn early on that was too complex, and you didn't need at the start?*
> *What would make it easier for you to find value from Asana?*

After asking all of these questions about their learning needs, we found that our customers really needed to understand how Asana was going to help them to solve a particular challenge rather than offer them a broad tool with wide application. A blank page for creating tasks was overwhelming, whereas a lesson and a template that promoted "Here's how you create an editorial calendar" was much more impactful.

We also found that collaboration was key to making Asana easy to adopt. Much like I imagine for the person who created the first

(continued)

walkie-talkie, it got a lot more fun once they convinced a friend to give it a try. We therefore did a better job earlier in the learner's lifecycle to encourage them to invite colleagues in. We provided content on super-easy collaboration, one-on-one team meetings, and effectively using communication tools that became the low-hanging fruit that helped us get people to start using Asana and forming habits.

Finally, we realized that a lot of the organizational challenges around adoption were due to change management. However great a product is, people will always struggle with changing their processes or onboarding a new system or new way of doing things. By starting at the earliest steps and curating a learning journey that walked them through their aha! moments, we could ease our customers' journeys.

Of course, the earliest steps might need defining, too. At Asana, we had assumed that the smallest step, creating a task, would be the optimal first learning opportunity for our customers, followed by creating a sub-task, and then a project. However, when we asked customers what order they would like to get content in, we realized that this wasn't effective, and that people don't work that way. First, a person will consider a project that they have to complete. They then break it down into smaller parts, tasks, and then smaller still, sub-tasks. When we switched this around, we found that we could guide customers to that aha! moment more quickly.

Using Aha! Moments to Reduce Time to Value

Once you've defined what success means for your product in each of your customer segments, create a learning journey to help the user get there faster. When done right, these learning journeys reduce your time to value (TTV). We talked a little about using TTV as an organizational metric in the last chapter, but let's go deeper.

Customer education teams often talk about TTV in the context of onboarding. When customers begin using a product, they're usually uncertain how (or even whether) it will benefit them. Then, they reach a pivotal moment where they say, *"Ah, this is how this tool is going to help me."* This is their first aha! moment. However, it's not the only one, and focusing on the first one alone can minimize the value of using aha! moments. The customer doesn't stop needing support or guidance once they have reached that initial understanding of how the product works; their need just changes. Without customer education as a guide, you're risking the user getting frustrated or churning, or taking a lengthy route to a simple fix and ending up way off course.

Instead, try leveraging aha! moments to map the whole customer journey. An effective learning journey will then guide users from one aha! moment to the next in the shortest possible time, helping them to gain the maximum amount of value in the least possible time throughout their lifecycle. At its core, this is what customer education is all about.

Be Mindful of the Mines: Don't Forget to Design for Pain Points, Too

There's a myth out there that a good product is always easy to use. If you've ever heard a product team say, "It's so intuitive, our users don't need education," you know what we're talking about. This myth is difficult to dislodge, and it doesn't do anyone any favors. The truth is: no matter how easy a product is to use, using a product effectively will almost always involve complexities. The product itself may have a very simple user interface; it might offer a streamlined product experience from the get-go. However, that doesn't mean that there isn't change management involved in getting users to do something differently than they ever have done before, or that there aren't going to be pain points and friction along the way to achieving success.

Part of your role as a customer education leader is to acknowledge those pain points and create an elegant design for these moments of frustration, just as much as you do for the aha! moments. Create a learning journey that actively targets that friction rather than ignoring it. When a customer predictably gets to that point, they will then have the tools they need to resolve it, and you can minimize the pain and frustration.

From Aha! to ROI: Aligning Customer Education with Customer Lifetime Value (LTV)

You can measure the success of your curated learning journey by following your TTV and correlating trained users with a reduction in the time taken to get there. But that's just part of a larger puzzle.

We looked at the benefits of using customer lifetime value (LTV) when we discussed creating brand ambassadors, but let's widen the lens and think about this metric in a much broader way. The goal of customer education is to provide customers with the maximum value so that they can do the best job possible using your product or service. The best way to measure the value you provide is with LTV. However, anyone who has used this metric knows – it's a hard calculation to get! It requires a lot of patience, relies on several variables, and is a lagging indicator, confirming trends or behavior after the fact rather than predicting ahead of time.

There's no doubt that you want to see a strong correlation between trained users and lifetime value. However, it may be easier to focus on reducing TTV as a strategy to get you there. Work on improving your ability to identify the aha! moments and streamline the journey for customers from one aha to the next. The more you can deepen that engagement for your users, the more likely you are to create champions and advocates, and boom – you'll find that you're increasing the lifetime value of your customers.

Your North Star – your aspirational goal – should be that your customers are getting the most value out of your product, and it makes sense to measure this by LTV. You want your users to see your solution as a mission-critical, integral part of their job. If you can make that happen, they'll renew their subscription, they'll expand their usage, they'll upgrade their package, and they'll tell their friends about you. These are all ways to incrementally increase the lifetime value of that customer. This process starts by understanding the job of each customer, defining their needs in segments, mapping their aha! moments, and then reducing TTV to get them there faster.

Eric Peters is the growth product manager at HubSpot Academy, and he discusses how HubSpot has widened the goals for customer education in order to better educate the market, below.

Thoughts from . . . Eric Peters, Growth Product Manager, HubSpot Academy

HubSpot has always made it a priority to *practice what we teach.* Inbound marketing is a strategy HubSpot has employed and taught for years that involves attracting, engaging, and delighting audiences with "remarkable" content in order to build trust and sign on long-standing customers. HubSpot Academy, HubSpot's integrated online course provider, is one demonstration of the inbound methodology, where we offer world-class online courses to the world for free.

The ways in which HubSpot Academy creates value for Hub-Spot have evolved over the years. The founding team was initially focused on building a scalable way to enable HubSpot customers to self-educate. They saw early on that it was going to be difficult to scale the services organization alongside rapid customer growth, and so they created recorded videos to help teach the basics of the HubSpot software platform. That's how it all began. Over time, what started out as recorded videos evolved, and eventually became certification courses, resulting in an ecosystem of "certified" experts around the HubSpot software.

As we released courses that taught business topics more broadly rather than only focusing on the tactical use of HubSpot software, our certification courses began to attract learners from around the world, introducing them to HubSpot with education. HubSpot Academy became part acquisition channel, part customer and partner enablement tool, with key metrics like content engagement, viewer retention, and qualitative feedback. Secondary metrics were the impact that each piece of content had on business KPIs like customer dollar retention and new user acquisition. These metrics could be applied to a wider range of use cases, whether the courses were teaching developers how to extend HubSpot through integrations, teaching HubSpot solution partners how to sell and serve our customers, teaching customers how to master HubSpot, or teaching university students about ad hoc topics like search engine optimization (SEO).

(continued)

We hold ourselves to the standards we teach in our courses, which say "solve for the customer." In terms of organizational design, our product team focuses on overall content engagement, while our content team focuses on the impact that individual courses have on their target audience within the HubSpot ecosystem.

Creating new content for HubSpot Academy always starts with learning outcomes. Of course, as we've grown, these outcomes are increasingly diverse and widespread and associated with different personas, experience levels, and buying journeys – but ultimately, this starts with the same idea. We drill down and think about what we want the user to do, what transformation we want them to have, and how that will create additional value for their customer. Let's say we want them to learn how to use the email tool within HubSpot. We think about what usage of this tool means for the customer, which is going to be higher deliverability or click-through rates and more engagement and trust building from their own customer. If our educational content solves for the customers of our customers, we can ensure that we're creating positive learning outcomes. This provides direct value to the HubSpot user and their business, and aligns their HubSpot product usage with their own business growth.

Educating the Market

One turning point for us at HubSpot was the introduction of product-agnostic content, and how we began using this strategy to teach users before they even become customers, effectively reaching out to educate the market. This has reduced the speed at which new customers can learn HubSpot and how quickly they can see value. For example, our marketing courses provide the methodology, the common language, and the strategic skills to use the platform even before they sign up, so they can hit the ground running and apply what they've learned if and when they do sign on as customers. These courses help people managers onboard new employees, they enable our HubSpot solution partners to assign training to new clients, and they build trust with our global audiences by helping them grow in their careers. In many cases, the best "customer support" for HubSpot isn't someone who works at HubSpot at all! Instead, it's the person sitting next to you who has taken one of our certification courses and knows your unique use case and your HubSpot implementation better than anyone else. That's the power of creating an ecosystem of experts.

Widening the Scope of Customer Education

I've seen over the years that because customer education typically lives on the customer success team, they tend to make the mistake of narrowing the scope and focus to simply teaching customers how to use their products. I believe that customer education has the power to do a lot more, if you can widen its scope and say, "Hey, let's help people build amazing careers," and then use your product as the means to get there.

There are so many experts out there who have created careers within software ecosystems. Think about the average tech employee resume, and the technologies listed in the technical skills section. From Adobe and Salesforce to Microsoft or SAP, technical skills are career-building skills. If you can create a world where your product is listed among these, you will have built a moat around your company that protects it from disruption. HubSpot has students in more than 1,000 universities around the world learning HubSpot software as part of their curriculum, and they come out of school knowing us, trusting us, and with experience in our product. That is very powerful. After all, especially in the SaaS world, it's easy to copy features from one product to another, but copying ecosystems is a whole lot harder. This starts with customer education, building trust at all stages of the customer lifecycle, from onboarding to mastery, and providing technical, tactical, and strategic skills that enable them to build amazing careers.

Designing with the customers' goal in mind, not focusing solely on your product but instead on the *value* that your product provides to your customers, is a foundational customer education principle. Now let's turn our attention to how we can work out what your customers practically need to know to realize that value.

5

Step 3: Personalize Learning by Focusing on What Your Customers Need to Know

At this point, you should have a good understanding of what your customers' jobs are and, therefore, how they define success. Now, here you are, ready to determine what they need to know to make that success happen.

Creating Effective Learning Personas

Before you start creating your content, you may want to think about your customers' different learning personas. While we've already discussed customer profiles, which allow you to segment users by their roles or their industries, learning personas will help you to segment your customers by their learning needs, and target the gaps in their knowledge – the things they need to learn in order to achieve their goals.

A learning persona is essentially a fictional profile that you develop that captures any segment of your customer base for whom you're designing a learning program. These fictional profiles should capture common characteristics from varied types of learners and are a great tool for breaking out of your own way of thinking and considering the learning journey from your customer's point of view. They can also be easily shared across teams and departments to help explain education content strategy and the type of customer that you're talking to, which is useful when liaising with various stakeholders in the business.

The characteristics you profile for a learning persona could be the kind of job they're trying to do, their goals, their background in terms of fluency or skill level with your product, the way they like to learn, or their experience with this kind of hardware or technology. You might decide to give the profiles or personas a name or some pictures that can really bring them to life. The goal of these profiles is to help you to recognize what kind of learning will resonate with the different customers who use your product, what their hesitations might be, and to support you in stepping into their shoes to get to know them and what they need to feel successful.

Are You an Eager Esther or a Reluctant Ray? How We Used Learning Personas at Asana

Let's take a look at three of the learning personas that we used at Asana. These can help you to understand how to capture common characteristics in a meaningful way. In turn, you can then use these kinds of profiles to create effective learning journeys that work for different segments of your own customer base.

First up, we have Eager Esther. She already knows a lot about project management, and she may already have experience with Asana, too. She's definitely used project management software in the past, and she has really specific learning needs that she's looking to fill. Get her on the phone with a customer support rep and she might ask, "How can I supercharge my editorial calendar?" or some other really specific query. She's kicking the tires of Asana, trying it on for size. If you approach Eager Esther with high-level content around what a project management tool does, you're going to lose her.

Next, meet Lost Lucy. She knows that something has to change, but she really doesn't know what. Work is falling through the cracks, collaboration is breaking down, people are missing deadlines, and there's rife miscommunication in her department and maybe even across the organization. But Lucy doesn't know how to use project management tools. She doesn't even know why they would be any better for her than a spreadsheet. She comes to Asana and signs up, and she needs someone to explain to her how it's going to provide value and help her with her day-to-day challenges. Here, you need to start your customer education earlier. Lost Lucy's education journey will start with empathy toward her problem, then cover what project management tools can do, providing foundational knowledge that helps her to see Asana as a solution before diving into any actual use cases.

Last, let's introduce Reluctant Ray. You might have thought that Lost Lucy and Eager Esther were like night and day, but the truth is they have a lot in common. They have a mutual recognition that they have challenges to solve, and they are both interested in solving those problems. Reluctant Ray is different. He wasn't looking to join Asana, or use any project management tool whatsoever. He's been invited to the platform by a colleague, or told that he needs to start using it by his manager. He already has his existing system in place, and even if it's a stack of Post-it notes, he feels strongly that it works completely fine. According to Reluctant Ray, there's no space for any new tools in his life. For this customer, education is really about change management. You need to start by convincing him that there's something wrong with the way that he is currently working, and then prove that there is a better way of doing things. Unlike Eager Esther and Lost Lucy, he isn't intrinsically motivated, so you might have to tap into another way to get him on board, such as gamification.

It's important to acknowledge that when you create learning personas, you're looking to capture the bulk of your learning needs, but you won't get them all. That's not realistic, and it also isn't helpful. These learning personas need to be broad enough to capture the types of needs that your customers have as much as possible, but still be easily distinguishable from one another.

How to Gather Information to Create Learning Profiles

Just like with understanding what your customers' goals are, the simplest way to gather information about your learners and their experiences is to ask them! As already mentioned, that means if you don't currently have a source of data that will help you to understand the different needs of your customers, create it. Send out surveys to your customers, or add an onboarding step where you explicitly ask customers the key questions that will help you sort learners into different categories. Examples could be, "We'd like to personalize this experience for you; have you ever used this kind of product before?" or "Were you invited to use this product by a member of your team, or are you looking for a solution for your own team?"

You may be able to augment this information with demographic data such as their job title or conversations that they have had with your sales team that shed light on their needs.

If your product itself doesn't have the functionality you need, use your LMS. At Thought Industries, we offer adaptive learning paths. The very first time a customer lands on your academy, you can ask a few questions. The answers to these will help you to channel learners into the right journey. This is a great example of an explicit data stream, something we'll examine later in this chapter. However you go about determining what your customers need to know, whether it's through creating learning profiles or not, remember that your goal is to get some awareness around why customers are hiring your product so that what you teach them aligns with what they need to learn.

Defining Common Use Cases for Your Product

One way to get to the core of your product's value proposition is to think about very specific common use cases. This can also help you avoid one of the most common mistakes that leaders make when creating customer education: making it all about the product.

If you try to teach your customers everything there is to know about how to use the product, you might think you're giving them the tools to do whatever they want with your technology or hardware, but you're actually making it harder for them to adopt your product in a meaningful way. By filling your customer education with "how-to" content or tutorials, you're relying on the users to make a cognitive leap to make your product applicable to their job. They might learn how to use a certain feature, click the right button, or set up some hardware, but that doesn't mean they know how to use your product to perform their role more effectively. In contrast, if you define common use cases that customers regularly leverage your product to accomplish, you're starting with something that aligns directly with the problems your customers are hoping to solve. As a result, your customers are bought into the process and invested in the outcome before they think about the fact that they're also learning the mechanics.

At Thought Industries, we provide a flexible platform with a lot of features and functionality, and our customer education is centered on how customers can use these features in vastly different ways. Many of our customers are SaaS businesses who need "academies" to teach their users how to use their software. However, we also have many professional training companies who use our platform to package and sell courses and professional associations who invite members to join and gain continuing education units (CEUs). In other words, how customers use our platform varies, depending on their use case, and so our approach to teaching them how to use our platform must vary as well.

Sandra Elliott, who leads customer education at Thought Industries, created learning personas to help us distinguish these differences. "Before we define what learners need to know," she said, "we first need to understand how they plan to use our product and to what ends." If we know how you intend to use Thought Industries, then we can customize the learning experience for you to help you achieve success more quickly.

How to Use the 80/20 Rule in Customer Education

Just like with creating learning profiles, you can't encompass everything and everyone in the education that you create. Especially if you have a complex product, there will always be edge cases, and people have emergent patterns that you may not have even considered when you designed the product in the first place! It's important to realize that it isn't only unrealistic to try and cover all the use cases, it's also not *desirable*. If you try to teach everything, you're going to create cognitive overload in your users, and your learners will begin to "check out." Even if a learner dutifully completes all of your training, the forgetting curve will kick in and wipe out most of that knowledge. Not everything will be relevant for every customer, or at every stage of the journey, so don't teach customers everything!

When it comes to creating your customer learning content, the 80/20 rule applies. Also known as the Pareto principle, the 80/20 rule asserts that 80 percent of outputs result from 20 percent of inputs. If you think about all of the content that you could create, you should consider that 80 percent of what your customers *actually* need to know in order to gain value from your product is likely confined to 20 percent of what you might teach them. The rest – 80 percent of that knowledge – is mostly applicable to edge cases or troubleshooting. Producing and teaching all of that content is not only time-consuming, it will also net you incrementally fewer gains overall. Instead, you should be focusing on the most useful 20 percent of your content – the stuff that matters – and make that content as polished and compelling as possible. You can see an example of this "80/20" rule, in Figure 5.1. That's not to say that you can't create ways to address those edge cases, but consider other formats that scale more easily. For example, a customer community can provide an excellent channel for customers to get answers to their relatively nuanced questions.

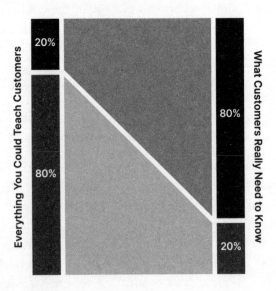

Figure 5.1 80/20 Rule

If you can honor this 80/20 rule, and isolate the real-life use cases that your different learning personas are looking to hire your product to fill, you're putting the value proposition of your solution front and center. You can then position your education to give customers what they want to know – namely, how they can utilize your product to improve how they do their job.

Using Data to Determine What Your Customers Need to Know

Up until now, we've talked about using instructional design work such as surveys and questionnaires to create learning personas and uncover use cases to create the right content for your customer education program. Of course, it can definitely help to back this up with data. In particular, you can leverage data to uncover two things:

1. *The proficiency of your users and how skilled they are at using your product, which includes their level of maturity.* Are your customers leveraging all the features that they could be to solve the problem they're trying to solve? With this information in hand, you can design a better learning journey. For example, if they're already skilled at using your product, you can give them more advanced content than if they're a new user. If they aren't using a specific aspect of your solution that could help them to achieve their goals, you can target them with education that explains its value, or if it's a premium feature at a higher tier, suggest an upsell.

2. *The friction that your customers are facing.* Where are they experiencing pain, or hitting walls? Without a clear view of this, it's going to be impossible to design a learning experience that mitigates that pain and helps them to push through it.

Explicit versus Implicit Data Sources

You can access this information through both explicit and implicit data sources, and most likely a mixture or triangulation of the two. Explicit data is exactly that – data that is provided intentionally and directly by your end users. It is clear, and without ambiguity. It requires little to no analysis to extract meaningful information from this data. Think about customer satisfaction surveys, support tickets that describe moments of friction, community threads, registration forms, or statements of goals. This is where your customers are literally telling you things – so listen up!

Implicit data is more common, but trickier to leverage. This data usually needs some analysis to make sense of. Take a look at your support documentation, for example. How often are specific help articles being accessed, and how highly are they being rated? If an article is visited often but rated as unhelpful, update it. On the other hand, if an article has a high rating but is underutilized, promote it. Next, look at your product analytics data. Where are people dropping out or churning? Which features aren't being used? Consider the terms that are most regularly being dropped in your website search bar, or at what point they're hitting the help button. With this information, you can target learning to boost engagement at the points of friction, or highlight the features that aren't being picked up, especially if they're directly aligned with specific use cases that your customers want to use your product to complete.

Connecting Back to Your Aha! Moments

Last, let's think back to our conversation about time to value. If you've defined your aha! moments accurately, this can also inform what you need to teach to achieve success for your customers, and reduce that TTV.

Let's say that your product is an email marketing software. You know that your customers' first aha! moment is when they send out a campaign and view the analytics. They can see the open rate, the click-through rate, and more. This is the moment they say, "Wow, this is a valuable tool! It's really going to help me to do my job." Knowing this, you can analyze all the users who reach this moment for patterns emerging in their behaviors. You now know that all the users who reach this moment complete these behaviors or these clusters of behaviors. In contrast, by looking at the actions of the churned users, you also know that those who *didn't* reach this aha! moment *haven't* done these same behaviors. So, essentially, what you've uncovered are a sequence of specific steps that you want to teach your customers, nurturing them from one to the next with clear calls to action.

Boom, you've just uncovered your curriculum, and you're ready to start planning out your content.

Lisa Rothrauff is the director of customer education at Amplitude, and she has also served in the same role at Zendesk. Her thoughts on determining what the customer needs to know to achieve success are included here.

Thoughts from . . . Lisa Rothrauff, Director, Customer Education, Amplitude

Wherever I work, I find it fundamental to understand as early as possible who our customers are and what role they play in their company. Do they have a team? What are they looking to achieve by using our products – and essentially, what are their goals? Do they want to improve efficiency on a team, or unlock a greater ability to scale? Are they an administrator focused on making the work for their agents easier or more pleasurable, or a team-leader looking to improve CSAT scores? Usually it's a combination, and sometimes it's all of the above.

My team then uses this information to create training that helps customers realize success. We try to put ourselves in the learner's shoes as much as possible. When I worked at Zendesk, our training used to be focused on the product itself and its features, and we would offer courses organized by product name. Later, the customer education team began to shift its approach and now frame the training within the context of our learner's job. Content is now being redesigned into learning paths where each learning experience is framed with relevant context for the customer. Instead of saying, "Learn How to Use Zendesk Support," it might say, "Learn How to Make Your Team More Efficient with Zendesk Support." Once the team has understood what's motivating people to use Zendesk, every module in the learning path is focused on that overarching goal.

(continued)

My Process for Understanding What Customers Need to Know

Wherever I work, to uncover what the customers need to know to reach any specific goal, we need to be resourceful in tapping into both the data we can access and the expertise across the company. I like to partner with internal teams across the business, from Product Marketing and Product to Sales and Customer Success, all of whom have a lot of deep product and customer knowledge. We also look at ticket data, starting with the overarching trends, and ask which topics generate the most tickets. We do the same thing with our documentation, reviewing those articles that are viewed most within a given time frame. We also leverage product engagement dashboards from our data team to see which features are used most and in which combinations by customer segments. Once we have captured that anecdotal evidence from customer-facing teams and reviewed the available data, we sometimes return to the internal teams who have the most intimate knowledge of our customer sets to validate the conclusions we have drawn. As a result, there's a constant cycle of speaking with account management teams, looking at data, and then coming back to the customer-facing teams for more nuanced insight.

Making Time to Consider What Not to Do

As well as teaching customers what they need to know to achieve success as they define it, customer education also supports by being transparent and by telling them what *not* to do. There are many ways to use any given product, but that doesn't mean they are all recommended. For example, there are common pitfalls that occur if the customer moves too quickly or sets up the product in a specific incorrect way. Over time, behind the scenes, we get wiser and wiser about what not to do, through repeat tickets or from interviews with the advocacy or success teams. We'll see a repeated challenge where customers disable a certain feature in order to customize a workflow, for example; yet by disabling that feature, they're causing challenges for themselves down the road. They would have no reason to know that of course, so we use education to preemptively help them avoid such mistakes.

We're often asked how we decide what to focus on and how we prioritize. Generally, we try to teach to 80 percent of the population, finding recurring patterns and common challenges and goals. Reminding our instructional designers of this helps us to stay focused on common use cases, keep to the critical path, and avoid overload for our learners. It's natural for us to want to share what we find interesting, but we need to manage our own curiosity and not get carried away by that. Sometimes in the comments on a help center article, in a community thread, or even anecdotally from success or services colleagues, we'll hear about edge cases. But it's essential to stay true to the customer voice and the customer need.

Thinking about Customer Maturity Levels

In some ways, we ask the same mentality from our customers. Whether they are admins, agents, or developers, we try to pace our learning for the customer and set expectations that they shouldn't be looking to certify straightaway. Just because they can access all our on-demand resources from the start, that doesn't mean it's wise to consume everything early in their journey. They need to acquire and validate their expertise, which happens over time and requires more than simply taking a four-hour workshop. It's about really using the product and getting familiar with it, starting with courseware, and then prep courses, and above all, getting in a lot of hands-on practice.

As we develop our curriculum, we also reference the concept of *spiraling*. For us, this means understanding not just what the customer needs to know but when they need to know it and how we can build their understanding of a concept and its application over time. You can introduce a concept in a simple way, and that could be enough

(continued)

for a first learning path. At another point, you can revisit the same concept in a new context or in a more applied or challenging way to underscore its applicability or malleability. It's an important message for instructional design teams to recognize – they don't need to teach everything at once, nor should they. As customers become more mature, they will develop their knowledge of a product more deeply and can see the kernel of a concept being carried through in different contexts. Think about the longer learning trajectory and balancing what needs to happen now, versus what you can trust will happen later. In that way, you and your team will be able to get a lot more focused about what you're providing in a single moment.

By personalizing learning to what the customer needs and setting a goal to support the learner with a journey to reach their own aha! moments, you can start building a picture of exactly what to cover in your education. To make sure it checks all the right boxes and minimize friction in its creation, in the next chapter we'll look at how to create an effective development plan.

6

Step 4: Execute Your Strategy Flawlessly with a Development Plan

Imagine for a moment that your company has just made a big announcement. This could be investing in a new product line, launching a new application, or building out a new department. For any truly mature project, you would expect there to be a thorough business plan.

Your customer education deserves the same focus and credence. That means it's not enough to define your goals, or even your customer's goals, and then just start training. You need a customer education development plan.

Your plan should include a complete project brief, which you can provide at the outset, and allows you to get cross-functional alignment on all the different stakeholders who will be developing customer education with you. To do that, you need to be able to show them a brief that answers at least the following questions:

Who is the customer education for?
What are you educating them on?

When do customers receive this education?
Where do they receive it?
Why have you chosen this approach, including why should the learners care?
How will you measure whether the education has had the intended impact?

When your stakeholders read this project brief, it should be enough to orient them so that they understand the goals and the focus of the customer education program, as well as how you're going to align to get there and how you will ultimately measure its success.

Identifying Your Stakeholders

Of course, you need to know who is being given this project brief. Defining this is an essential part of your development plan. Here, you need to consider who is going to be involved in which elements of the education program as a whole and in each specific task.

One option is to use the RASCI model, which is a variant of the RACI model, a project management tool that originally came from software development. When used effectively, a RASCI matrix can help you to identify all the stakeholders who will be involved on any given project and assign their roles and responsibilities in a clear and shareable way.

Here's how it works and how it can be used to identify stakeholders for a customer education project and to manage the project efficiently as it evolves.

Start by writing down everyone who will be involved in the customer education program and figuring out in what way they would need to be involved. Then mark up how they will be involved by splitting the program down into smaller tasks, from planning and analysis, to design and customization, and iteration or support:

Responsible.
If you're *responsible* for a particular task, that means that it's your duty to get that job done. You can think about this role like a project owner. More than one person can be responsible for any given task, and they will need to consider how to split their responsibilities.

Accountable.

The buck stops with you. You have control over how the task is done, including what resources to allocate, the time frame, and – if delegation is necessary – who you make responsible for any specific subtasks or elements of the project.

Supportive.

If you're supportive in a certain task, you may be called on by those who are responsible for the task to help with a particular element of the project. This could be due to time constraints, specific experience or expertise, or just the need for an extra pair of hands.

Consulted.

You may be assigned as consulted on a specific project or task if you're a subject matter expert or have relevant expertise that can help get a project through to completion.

Informed.

These are stakeholders who simply need to be kept in the loop. They will not formally contribute to the tasks involved in the project, but they need to be kept aware of what's going on, including if timelines, scope, or budget changes from the original plan.

The RASCI Model in Practice

Let's look at a practical example of RASCI used in customer education. In this scenario, your company builds and sells electric wheelchairs, and your customer education program is aimed at helping your channel partners and distributors sell this product to their own customers, your end users.

You may have several project managers who are responsible (R) for creating the education, all of whom are accountable (A) to the executives who need to know that your material is high quality and accurate. You then have supportive (S) stakeholders who might go onsite to deliver the education or speak to factory workers on behalf of the team. Consulted (C) subject matter experts would be those who understand granular compliance requirements or the machinery involved in the wheelchair itself, and informed (I) members could be on a C-suite level or cross-departmentally in sales or customer success.

Using the Matrix

Once you've created your matrix, take a critical look across each line. You might want to consider the following questions.

Is There the Right Number of Responsible People?   Too many, and you may find there is confusion over who is truly meant to take the initiative on that task. Too few, and tasks are unlikely to get done at all.

Is a Single Person Accountable for Each Task?   Every line needs just one person who is accountable for seeing the task through to completion. As this person will have the final say on whether a task is complete, more than one can slow down the process.

Will Some Roles Be Flexible?   Especially in the consulting or supporting role, you may want to assume that people will adapt as needed. For example, you may start out asking someone for advice in a consulting role, and instead they offer to become responsible for the task that needs to be done.

Is the Matrix Streamlined, but Complete?   Who doesn't want to fill an empty box? It can be easy to add roles and responsibilities just because they're open, but this can also add complexity or delay. Ensure you haven't missed anything essential, but don't add stakeholders for the sake of it.

Using the Project Management Triangle for Your Development Plan

Once you have identified stakeholders, it's time to develop your plan. We recommend leveraging the project management triangle (Figure 6.1), which is widely used in business planning. For our needs, we can define it as this: The quality of your customer education plan will be heavily impacted by

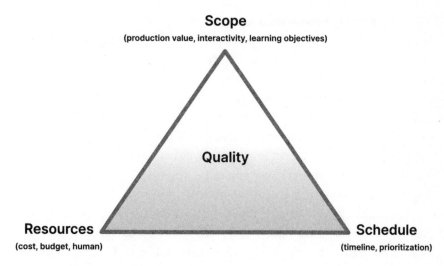

Figure 6.1 Project Management Triangle

the balance between the scope of your project, the timeline you have for it, and the resources that you have in place.

The three corners of the project management triangle need to be considered at the start of your development plan, then realigned every time a change is made. For example, if your timeline suddenly moves forward, you may need to think again about the scope of the project or whether you can find additional budget to make it happen faster. If your budget is cut, you might look to see if you can push back the deadline or adjust the scope to fit the resources you have. If one or more of these are out of balance, it can negatively impact the quality of your customer education as a whole. Let's look at each of these in more detail.

Establishing Scope

Defining the scope of your project can be much more difficult than it sounds, as a customer education program often starts with a vision that's in a person's own head. This vision could be fuzzy at first, and you need to learn how to communicate the plan to your eLearning designers and the other stakeholders on your team. There are a few good questions to start with, though.

First, how high production does this need to be? As part of the scope, think about whether you need to create a professional learning experience with a high production value, or whether this is something you can whip up with a webcam. Think about whether the "wow" factor is a necessary part of this education, or if you can be just as effective with less production and pizzazz, and get the project done in less time and with fewer resources. I'm a real advocate for making sure that the scope of your project is focused, tight, and not overproduced. Your scope will have a direct impact on your timeline and your resources, so if you can reduce the production value here, you'll be able to go further with time, people, and budget.

Sometimes, after thinking about it, the answer will be that you definitely need that wow factor, and that's fine! An example could be if the goal of your program is to improve brand awareness. Then, of course, you want to be more mindful of professionalism and production value. However, if in another example, you're looking to create a tutorial video on a product feature that will likely evolve or change, you may not need all of the bells and whistles: a simple screencast will do.

Great advice is to always lean toward getting something out rather than let perfection become the enemy of progress. As creators, we can feel tempted to keep iterating, improving, and making things as good as possible. However, no one will argue with you that the quicker you can get something to market, the better. Work out what the necessary level of quality is for it to be ready for its audience, and stick to that. This may be a good time to think about whether there is any content that you can reuse to avoid any redundant work. One of the first things we ask when starting a new learning experience is, "What do we have that already covers this?" It's helpful to take an audit of all the existing content so that when you plan to launch something new, you know whether something already exists that you can leverage to your advantage.

Second, think about the level of interactivity that you're going to create. The more interactive your content, the longer it will take to produce, and therefore the higher the cost. At one end of the spectrum, you have simple text or graphics-based content where the learner clicks and reads before moving onto the next stage. At the other end of the spectrum, if your content is considered highly interactive, it will include more complex branching scenarios and nonlinear navigation options, so that the user can move around the content in a personalized way according to their needs. When determining the level of interactivity, consider whether it's in service of your learning goals, and if the incremental gains in learning outweigh the added production cost. Also, be mindful of audience expectations; some audiences will want an engaging and interactive experience, while others might find it annoying because it slows them down.

The third question you can ask yourself when identifying scope is, how many problems are you trying to solve with your education? Ideally, your learning experience should address one objective, so focus on a single topic. It's also important to remember that the best learning experiences will be modular, so that you have many disparate eLearning opportunities that all individually address a single topic and come together to form a whole. This is easier for so many reasons. On the back end, modular eLearning means you have a greater ability to make changes on the fly and to reuse modules for other purposes. For the customer, they gain the ability to learn to their own preferences as well as the benefits of doing different learning tasks in different ways, where the novelty helps solidify the learning.

ADDIE versus SAM – Does It Matter?

There are two common ways of running a project that are brought up a lot in learning methodologies and touted as potential ways to create an educational experience. ADDIE is an acronym for Analyze, Design, Develop, Implement, Evaluate. SAM stands for Successive Approximation Model. At their core, these are both project management methodologies that have been applied to instructional design. ADDIE is often compared to the Waterfall model of software development, where you complete each stage one after another, while SAM is usually seen as more iterative or compared to Agile.

In our opinion, there's nothing about the stages involved in ADDIE that stops you from being iterative about the process if you're designing an eLearning experience. All you need to do is add iterative steps into the project! Many people have suggested adding

(continued)

elements of Rapid Prototyping or a more cyclical approach to this methodology to make it more agile, and that's great! Remember that these are both just methodologies, and you don't need to be wedded to any particular framework. Look at your project, your stakeholders, your learners, and your own preferences, and take inspiration from where it comes!

Setting a Timeline

In some cases, you may find that the timeline for your customer education program is led by the go-to-market (GTM) strategy of the company more widely. It's important to make sure that you have a plan in place that meets the pace of evolution of the product and its release cycle. Often, the product teams release a new feature or an update to an existing product, and the customer education team find themselves playing catch up. They may have to rush to get content out there that helps the customers to use a new update, or worse still, reactively amend existing content to meet a change. We'll talk more in Chapter 9 about making sure that you can get a seat at this particular table.

Whether or not your timeline is your own, rather than simply picking or aligning an ultimate completion date for your customer education program, it can be helpful to break down your project into smaller parts and create milestones that you can check in on, iterate, and adjust as necessary.

Before you can create milestones, visualize what your project will look like upon completion. Once you have that picture in mind, then you should be able to work backward from there to work out the stages of what needs to be done to get to that end goal. Identifying milestones along the way is a great way to keep you on track and also to break up your work into smaller, digestible actions that give plenty of room to iterate along the way.

Let's say that you're identifying the end result as a full-blown academy course on customer onboarding. Your milestones could be something like this:

1. Identify learning objectives, including the modules that will be included in the course.
2. Flesh out what a learner needs to achieve or know to meet each learning objective.
3. Talk to the relevant stakeholders who will be making the eLearning happen. Time to think RASCI.
4. Complete your instructional design work, from organizing and sequencing to presenting the content in an optimized way for learning. This will become your course design document.
5. Start developing this into a version one of your course, which may be as simple as a slide deck and some talking points.
6. Collect feedback and implement it in an iterative way without developing something sophisticated.
7. Develop your eLearning.

At each of these milestones you have an opportunity to gather feedback, identify the people in the consultative or supporting category, and check that you're getting the right input. Do all stakeholders agree with your plan? What do the relevant people think about the first draft of your learning? Ensuring the process is truly an iterative one allows you to constantly improve without needing huge changes that make a dramatic impact on what you've done so far. For example, after milestone 4, you can show a subject matter expert your outline, and ask them for their thoughts on how it's shaping up, before you even create that first "quick and dirty" version of your education.

Defining Your Resources

The last point on the project management triangle is your resources. It's important to recognize that you may find it easier to adjust a timeline or a scope than you will to make changes to the resources that you have. For example, a lot of professionals working in customer education are a team of one or two. These small teams are being asked to do a lot of things, and they don't have a lot of control over their resources to make that happen.

We discussed above about starting with the scope of your project, being as focused as possible, and then using this metric to work out your resources in terms of cost or people. In many cases, you might want to turn this on its head and start by understanding what resources you have, then working backward to build out the scope and the timeline.

When you're assigning these resources to your project, think back to what we said earlier about leaning toward a bias for action. As learning professionals, of course, we want to ensure that our experiences are effective and engaging and a great learning experience. But it's important to remember that we're doing this in the service of customers who need this content for the value that it provides and don't care about the package it comes in. Whirlpool doesn't need to create a 30-minute tutorial video about how to repair a dishwasher because a customer has already uploaded a 7-minute video to YouTube that gets the job done. In general, customer education professionals tend to default to a higher level of quality than they need to, and if you are cognizant of this, you may be able to do more with less.

Managing the three points of your triangle can be a bit of a puzzle. In most cases, you'll find that at least one of the points is fixed, such as a timeline where you need to meet a specific product release, or the resources in a team of one. In these cases, that will heavily impact the scope of your project.

When you have a budget in mind, the puzzle becomes a little clearer to manage. You may find that using this budget, you can fold contractors into your projects, which in turn can help you to increase the level of production value or interactivity for your content. Contractors are a wonderful resource if you can use them, expanding a small team to do a lot more than they could manage in-house.

To build out a budget, you need to be able to estimate the cost of your customer education. Estimating cost can be tricky, but you get better at it the more content you create. Start by thinking about how long it's going to take to create an hour of viewing content. This will depend on the elements we discussed when you were establishing scope, the interactivity of the content, and the level of production. As a general rule, for the simplest form of content, with low interactivity and the lowest possible production value, this is about an hour for each minute that you create, a ratio of 60:1. Scale your content up to the highest level of production value, and the most interactivity, and it could be 10 times that amount, 600 hours for a single hour of content.

It's not just important for you to have a sense of how long it's going to take to create content — it's also important to be able to communicate that to your stakeholders. There's a common fallacy out there that if someone takes a 30-minute course, that translates to a day or two of work for the customer education team to complete behind the scenes. However, creating a learning experience is not the same as building a slide deck. Instructional design is a craft, and there are a lot of steps to take before you can create something that will ensure effective learning.

Debbie Smith, customer education leader and head of Smartsheet University, shares her thoughts on creating an impactful customer education development plan.

Thoughts from . . . Debbie Smith, Head of Smartsheet University

When working on a new plan for customer education, there are two options, depending on how quickly you need to get content out and what your initial goal is.

No matter which goal you are working toward, one of the most important things to be aware of is that all training is customer focused and not feature focused. Training needs to be created based on the customer needs. If the goal is to solve for "How do I?" questions and to reduce support tickets, then I pull the most-often-asked questions from the CRM or support team and prioritize a list of videos to solve for this. However, if the goal is onboarding or a formal education program, then I like to create a Job Task Analysis (JTA) and, if time permits, a JTA survey. A JTA can be completed in a couple of days if you have the right SMEs in the process. This is a foundational stage in your customer education plan that lists all the tasks and knowledge that someone needs to know when using your product. If this is all the time that you have, you can start to develop content and then do a JTA survey.

It can take about two months to create a JTA survey from scratch, including getting internal buy-in, collecting the responses,

(continued)

and analyzing the data, but once this is complete, it can be incredibly powerful in helping your team focus on the customer outcomes instead of on your product.

If you can do the survey, then you send three questions to your customers:

1. How hard is this task to do?
2. How often do you do this task?
3. How important is the task to your role?

Using a JTA survey is a really clear way of working out what you should be focusing on, providing a full picture of the customer's needs in relation to your product. It can help you to prioritize the order of content creation for education and where your team should focus with the voice of the customer in mind.

With the answers to your survey, you can stack rank everything that you need to create by what's critical for the customer, and this is actually one of the easiest ways to organize and develop a roadmap while keeping the balance of time, scope, and budget in mind. For example, if something is very important to your customers and hard to do –, this naturally leaps to the top of your roadmap. However, if you see that this only impacts a small sub-section of your customer base, or that they perform the task sporadically and it is not an important task, perhaps it can be moved down the list, and replaced with something that's more important, used more often, or harder to do. If all of your customers are finding something easy, this doesn't have to be a focus at all.

Don't forget to ask your partners and your employees to fill out the JTA survey, so that you can look at the differences between the answers. Often this is where some really cool insights surface – showing the parts of the product that customers find easy to use that your employees assume is complex, or the knowledge that partners skim over where actually your customers would like to see more support or guidance.

From RACI to RASCI

When creating a customer education development plan, traditionally I would lean on the RACI model to identify and manage stakeholders, but I found that the person who was responsible wasn't always the person doing the work. In fact, in RACI, you often miss the person who is doing the work, such as an SME, a writer, or a video editor because the responsible person is a project or program manager. This is where the S for supporting comes in, making it the RASCI model. These supporting stakeholders can really make or break a project, so for me the addition has really improved the use of this model.

While it's fine to have as many informed and consulting roles as you need, remember to have just a single person accountable and a single person responsible. If you see that you have more than five people in a supporting role, this is likely a sign that the project needs to be broken down into smaller deliverables. I like to create multiple tiers with one high-level milestone, and then smaller deliverables underneath to keep things manageable and clear.

Choosing the Right Stakeholders

Now that you have deliverables organized, start thinking about who you need involved. As a customer education professional, you serve the needs of so many people, so bringing in stakeholders from different parts of the business is really important. I usually start with the internal stakeholders, then reach out to external partners. Of course, don't forget your customers! You should never create a project plan for customer education without getting customer input first. You can use surveys, speak face to face, or leverage email, but make sure that you collect the data to understand the customer's pain points.

Internally, I always want to pull in the product marketing manager so that I can include what's important to them, and I make sure that someone from customer success who speaks directly to the customers has a seat at the proverbial table, too. Software companies in particular often design software the way we think customers will

(continued)

use it, but CSMs are on the frontlines in terms of knowing what customers are actually doing. If you have solution architects or implementation consultants, draw on these people as a technical resource as they can provide invaluable insight into customer requirements.

Remember, when you first start a new customer education plan, or you're new in your role, you might not personally know all the right people. One thing that you can do is to ask your colleagues, "Who knows everything there is to know about this area? Who is the real OG?!" These people have been around since the early days of the company and have gathered all the tribal knowledge in terms of how things work the way they do, and why. Sometimes these stakeholders sit in unusual places. I've been in companies where someone in the procurement team, who I would never have thought to approach as an SME, was actually an ex-CSM who had worked in a customer-facing role for a decade and knew it all. At start-ups, especially, employees tend to move around the company, and if you can highlight the people with this tribal knowledge, it can be incredibly helpful.

Lastly, it's important to have a balance of SMEs who are product-focused and customer-focused people, but the goal of the training should not be product-focused. You want to make sure that when you're training, you're not explaining, "What can the product do?" but rather, "What can the customer do with this product?" It sounds like a subtle shift, but when you can encourage your stakeholders to make that mental switch, I've seen a real change in the value and impact of the training in terms of how effectively learning takes place.

Creating a customer education development plan helps to keep all stakeholders aligned on their responsibilities and communication from day one. It also forces you to start any customer education project by considering the time and budget you have at your disposal, which is of paramount importance before you start the next step – creating the content itself.

7

Step 5: Video or Course? Choosing the Right Content Format for the Job

It's time to consider the varying formats available to you and take some time to understand when you might want to use each one. This is really all about ensuring that you have developed a strategy for your content.

Remember first and foremost that learning is not a single event. It's a series of processes that will include multiple experiences over time, as the customer goes through a journey from awareness, to considering, to buying, to growing, and the many micro-stages in between. When you're thinking about creating these experiences, it can be helpful to consider the forgetting curve, shown in Figure 7.1.

The forgetting curve visualizes the way that learners respond to content, and the impact of practice and repetition on their retention and knowledge. As people often forget what you teach them, you need to consolidate their learning regularly, through spaced intervals of training. This can be made up of both macro- and microlearning.

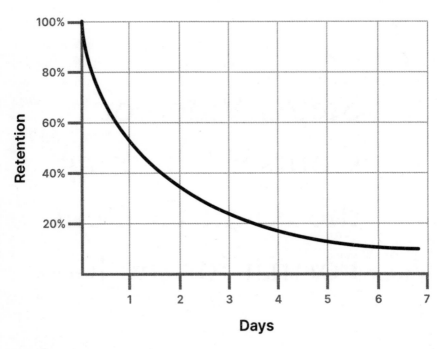

Figure 7.1 Forgetting Curve

Microlearning is designed to help in the moment and should be topic-based, usually taking two minutes or less. Examples could be short articles, images, or video clips. In contrast, macrolearning is designed to teach something larger, such as a new skill, and usually takes place over several hours or days. Examples of macrolearning are courses, learning paths, or instructor-led training. To meet customer needs, you will likely need to incorporate both at different stages. For example, you might begin with an onboarding course, and then supplement that over the following weeks with microlearning (videos, articles, emails, and so on) focused on the same topics in order to combat the forgetting curve. Then, after the learner has grasped the fundamentals, you can invite them to a more advanced course.

Blended, Hybrid, and Mixed-Mode Learning – Whatever You Call it, Mix It Up!

In general, learning works best when you use a wide range of formats. Traditionally, blended learning refers to any educational content where a student experiences both classroom-based and online learning as part of the experience. You may also hear terms such as *hybrid learning* or *mixed-mode* used to discuss different formats of online and in-person or instructor-led learning coming together to form a whole. For want of a more precise term, and for the purposes of this conversation, when we talk about blended learning here, we're describing the mixing of different formats of training and content to reach a deeper level of learning, whether that's online and offline, macro- and microlearning, or self-paced and instructor-led. Regardless of what you call it, understand that the optimal approach, if you want your customers to reach a level of mastery sustained over time, is to mix up different types of learning formats.

Blended learning allows you to get the best of both worlds. On the one hand, you can provide a personalized online learning experience using personas, as we discussed earlier, and offer the accessibility and convenience of self-paced learning online so that your learners can work at their own pace. On the other, you can use in-person or instructor-led courses that allow you to broaden the learner experience and provide more hands-on support, both from an expert instructor and from other learners, which is awesome for collaboration. Because of this, recent studies have shown that mixed modalities such as blended learning can have a strong impact on long-term learning achievement and retention.[1]

Optimize to Scale for Production

As touched on earlier, part of your content strategy is making sure that you are able to produce content within the constraints of your budget and your timeline. That's why one of the smartest things a team can do is to create templates for content creation, speeding up the process of creating educational content. If your team is small and you're being asked to do a lot, this practice is even more important. Your template could be as simple as a document that you can share with your subject matter experts or instructional designers where you outline everything that needs to go into a specific type of content. Once you've created the first one, you can then quickly switch

---

[1] C. Şentürk, "Effects of the blended learning model on preservice teachers' academic achievements and twenty-first century skills," *Educ Inf Technol* 26, 35–48 (2021), https://doi.org/10.1007/s10639-020-10340-y.

out the parts that need changing. When you're using a customer learning platform like Thought Industries, being able to create content from a template is so much easier than starting from scratch every time. For articles, this template might include all the HTML or code required for the design or formatting, while for case studies it could have your company boilerplate and a formatted space for a quotation or a statistic. As you get better at templating over time, you'll create blueprints that allow you to produce and scale your content production cycle more quickly.

One example of how we optimized education at Asana was for our "What's new at Asana?" videos. We knew that we wanted a new video each month, so Carla Bagdonas, Asana's Customer Education Program Lead, spent a single day shooting as much content as possible, including 20 versions of the intro and outro in 20 different outfits while repeating the same duplicate content 20 different times. Then each month, she'd add the right screencasts and augment with a simple recorded voiceover as needed. As a result, we dramatically reduced the amount of time and money that we spent in the recording studio.

Creating Modular Content

How many of us have had to trawl through an hour-long course that tries to cram 10 topics into a single piece of education? This is not only hard on the learners, but also not practical for customers. Your customers are busy people, and the last thing they want to do is take an hour from their day to find out the one thing they want to know by searching through 20 pieces of content.

On top of this, if you create an hour-long course on your product and then a feature changes, it becomes extremely difficult to maintain. Today, with an agile product cycle, you may have updates as often as every few weeks, and you just won't be able to keep up.

Instead, a modular content strategy will help you create focused learning content that has a single learning objective or topic. These modules can then be assembled into chunks that make sense to achieve a larger learning outcome. A modular approach gives you a lot of flexibility to serve multiple purposes, as a huge amount of content can be created from the same modules put together in different combinations. As standalone modules, content can be distributed in-product or leveraged on social media. Together, they become a macrolearning experience like a course or a way to teach a new skill. Modular content is also more digestible, and it is usually highly relevant because it's focused and short. This means your customers are far more likely to consume it.

Modular content is a key part of reinforcement. It is easy to strategically surface at spaced intervals to combat the forgetting curve, and it's much easier for customers to find again when they can't remember how to do something. After all, if it's too hard for customers to find the support that they need, they simply won't look.

On the business side, modular content is also much easier to maintain. Instead of starting from scratch with an entire course, you can simply switch out small parts as your product evolves or is updated with new features. A good example would be the difference between creating a fully designed PDF workbook for new users to learn about how to use your product, compared to using a slide deck with screenshots and instructional guidelines. The slide deck is much more modular, allowing you to switch out specific slides without impacting the whole, while a workbook would need to be reproduced every time a small change is made.

There are two techniques for creating a modular content strategy. If you're creating from scratch, you can simply start by making bite-sized pieces of content and then assembling them into bigger chunks as necessary. However, if you're reading this and suddenly realizing that all of your content is in long-form, it's not too late! In fact, sometimes it's easier to start with something like a webinar, test it, collect questions, and refine the content and then break it down into meaningful chunks for microlearning.

Defining Format According to Your Goals

It's important to choose a format for your content that aligns with your original strategy from step one. Defining conventions across your team and then being consistent is essential. Let's look at some of the formats you could choose, and the goals they best align to.

Help Articles

These are written articles that usually have clear steps that explain product functionality. Often augmented by screenshots or even short video content, they can be used to demonstrate a complex way of doing things. Help articles focus on the mechanics of your product, and the customer will usually look for these when troubleshooting.

Articles are a great format if the goal of your customer education is to deflect support tickets or to scale your support team. A secondary goal could also be around helping your customers adopt your product, as product adoption is encouraged by a mix of surfacing value and providing in-product support.

In-Product Education

In-Product Education (IPE) surfaces learning contextually within your product and provides a way to offer additional support to guide learners to perform a task at the moment of need. This is also called just-in-time learning. Similar to help articles, it removes the pain point for the customer by offering support when they need it. If you are aware of specific elements of your product that can be difficult or cause friction, this kind of education is a great way to alleviate it.

IPE aligns well with deflecting support tickets and also with encouraging your users to adopt your product. One good use case can be for empty state features, where there is no data to display to the users yet. A blank page can be daunting for a customer, and they may not know what the feature is for. This is an opportunity to create a short video or infographic that explains how the feature will help them achieve their goals.

Another form of contextual learning that is gaining popularity for physical products leverages augmented reality. For example, you might load a learning app on your smartphone, open a course on a specific piece of machinery, and through the camera on our device, view labels of the different parts of the product, including tips and tricks on getting the most value.

Video Content

Let's look at two kinds of video content. First, the on-demand tutorial, a video usually done using a screencast. It may have a narrator, and it is a great format for teaching specific, complex procedural knowledge. These videos can be fairly long and include a workflow that requires multiple steps. Such a video can be used in place of (or in conjunction with) a long, written help article, as you may find that a video modeling each step in the process works a lot better for complex workflows.

The other option is a short, explainer video. These videos are more suitable for strategy or conceptual content. They are simple, engaging, and meaningful, and are used to illustrate ideas. Use explainer videos to create a mental model around the value of the product rather than explain procedural steps about its use. Our Feature Spotlight videos at Thought Industries are a good example of this kind of content. They are less about how to use the product and more about the value of the product and why it's useful.

Virtual Instructor-Led Training (VILT)

If you're hearing that your customer success team members are having the same conversations over and over again, a great format choice might be VILT. For example, a virtual training webinar that you can run at a regular cadence.

This format is especially good for focusing on the foundations that help people who are new to your product or for drilling down into a specific use case in your product. They allow users to get some extra attention from an instructor as well as learn from other attendees. It's also a helpful way to pilot new content and record it for on-demand viewing. If you have an idea for a course that you want to create, try it as VILT first. Then you can iterate and test before you commit.

eLearning: Courses and Learning Paths

eLearning is probably one of the first things that come to mind when people think about customer education. A learning path is a cluster of courses that are usually sequenced in a way that guides the learner from one learning experience to the next, culminating in a summative exam that ensures that you've mastered the material. Many courses are tied together to allow you to master a broader subject or an entire program. Your learner can be nurtured from one course to the next without a lot of promotion to drive learners to an overarching goal. Better yet, make your learning path adaptive; if you have 10 courses in a learning path, you might offer learners an exam at the beginning that allows them to skip the first two courses because their level of mastery is slightly higher. You can also use adaptive learning paths for different learning personas; for example, everyone takes the first three courses, then learners take a specific track based on whether they work in marketing or sales, before being channeled back to the main path to conclude the learning journey.

Courses and learning paths are a very effective content format if you're looking to address complex material, drive engagement, and build mastery in your product. They are also necessary if you have a certification program as a way to prepare learners to take the assessment and pass it. If your goals are to create experts and advocates and train the trainers, then eLearning courses and learning paths are the way to go.

In our opinion, the optimal eLearning course is tightly focused on a small number of learning objectives, usually focused on a particular feature or use case or phase in the customer's journey like onboarding. It shouldn't be overly long, as that can negatively impact engagement and completion. Keep it less than 30 minutes, certainly no longer than an hour. In general, 10- to 20-minute courses are best to ensure a tight focus and to engage users for success, ending with an assessment of what they have learned. These short courses can then be strung together to create a learning path, which can be targeted for a persona. Let's say a persona is an admin, for example. You would want to set up a learning path that guides them through everything they need to know to successfully launch the product. This could include a number of courses, sequenced together in a way that facilitates deeper learning. When you reach the end of the learning path, you've completed multiple courses, and overall you've nurtured learners to achieve a broader, sizable goal.

Live Labs and Simulations

If you have a deeply complex software tool, or there are high risks involved in using the product incorrectly, then you may need hands-on training. Live labs are a format that allows you to create a simulated environment where you can train using realistic activities that mirror your product experience. This means that customers can make mistakes, mess around, and really test and play in a safe, isolated space. They are particularly effective in open-ended workflows, such as writing code. However, if we're thinking about our earlier trifecta of time, scope, and cost, it's important to remember that live labs are at the far end of the production scale in terms of resources, so you may need to factor that in.

On-Site Training

This is a format that is best leveraged for highly tailored premium training experiences. This format is a great option if you think that change management might be a potential issue and you want to nurture a relationship in a deeper way, generate enthusiasm, and create evangelists and advocates. Of course, it's not a scalable method of education, but this is a particularly viable option if you have an educational services function and you have a way to monetize some of your offerings. Many larger, enterprise organizations expect customized instructor-led training; if your company touts itself as "enterprise software," consider developing an on-site offering.

Job Aids

Job aids are also known as handouts or takeaways, and are physical documents that are printed out and used to consolidate knowledge, kept on hand to provide a reminder or refresher of training or education. There's something satisfying about completing education where you can walk away with more than just insight, but also a tangible takeaway that you can use to help you in your role. These are particularly helpful devices for driving additional engagement with your content, because who doesn't love a freebie or a takeaway? Let's say you're a customer education professional and you're taking a course on formats for customer education. You may get a printout with 10 types of content, and then three bullet points for each type of content. You can use this to deliver training yourself, print it out and pin it up in the office, or share with other colleagues. It's a versatile type of content that is great for role mastery.

Community

Whenever we think of community as a format, we think about an untapped gold mine. It's often untapped because it's not promoted widely enough or maintained, and it definitely needs nurturing for success. However, if you can successfully create a community, you're connecting customers with one another, giving new users an avenue to ask questions (some of them very nuanced questions for particular use cases), and giving evangelists a channel to advocate and express enthusiasm. It's such a wonderful recipe for sharing best practices and for scaling support. You will have help articles and education for the 80 percent of your content, the main use cases, but you're never going to cover every angle, and customers can really benefit from a place to ask about unconventional use cases and get answers from people with more experience. This can scale support, deflect support tickets, and provide brand advocates with an avenue to share best practices. Customer education teams should leverage community content more, pulling threads to create new content.

Daniel's Favorite Example of Community Content

A good example of community-driven content is an eBook I downloaded in my first week at Optimizely. It was called "Everything You Need to Know to Get Started but Didn't Think to Ask," and was essentially created from a community thread. The question that had been asked was, "What is something you wish you knew when you started that you know now?" Quickly, the thread became very long with a lot of great advice. The marketing team saw how valuable this information was and leveraged it by packaging it as an e-book. Customers who read it benefited from the wisdom of many others who came before them. Talk about a shortcut to aha! moments!

Microlearning

Highly focused and short, microlearnings can be consumed in small, digestible bites. This is a universally flexible and easy-to-produce format for all sorts of content. If you have a strategy that places microlearning front and center, you have created an omnichannel piece of content that can be placed in different formats and channels. It can be used in-product to help drive consumption, on social channels to promote awareness for marketing, and assembled together in a modular way to create longer course formats. Microlearning boosts the retention of knowledge by at least 20 percent.[2] As such, providing regularly spaced microlearnings is one of the most successful ways to combat the forgetting curve.

Assessments

Let's look at three types of assessments: formative, summative, and certifications.

Formative assessments are methods that instructors and eLearning designers use to check for understanding, evaluate comprehension in the moment, and reinforce learning by evaluating your knowledge. They are often a short quiz or a drag-and-drop assessment. The purpose isn't to test your knowledge, but to identify gaps for the learners in their own understanding and to reinforce the learning experience. They help students learn and practice. It works well to sprinkle these through the courses you create.

Summative assessments are more about assessing whether knowledge transfer has taken place and are given at the end of training to gather insight on performance and proficiency. These are effective at making sure that learning transference has occurred. Without summative assessments, you can't identify if your course has been effective or if it has been aligned well with your learning objectives. Use these to show both the learner and the business that the material has been mastered, rather than just the course has been completed. Most customers generally appreciate an opportunity to assess their own mastery at the end of a course.

Certifications are comprehensive summative assessments that usually take significant effort to design. For high-risk industries, such as

---

[2] L. Giurgiu, "Microlearning an evolving elearning trend," *Scientific Bulletin-Nicolae Balcescu Land Forces Academy* 22, 18-23 (2017).

cybersecurity, certifications signify trust and credibility, and so they're often taken more seriously. For example, they might require an independent proctor to monitor the exam. If your goal is to provide a signal for domain mastery, certifications are a great option.

Webinars

Think of webinars as a form of VILT, but rather than limiting participants and focusing on a deeper engagement level, a webinar gives you the opportunity to communicate information to an unlimited number of participants, whether live or prerecorded. Some people host a webinar live once and then make it available on-demand, while others may create a simulcast, where you're live answering questions, but you're hitting play on a prerecorded webinar. Webinars are an awesome way to pilot content. If you have a curriculum that you're working on, rather than spending all the time creating a multi-course learning path, run it as a webinar to test it out and see what your audience thinks before doing any more. It's also great for topics that are narrow, such as industry updates, thought leadership, or product updates. If you need to address a topic that is best addressed live because people may have questions about it, a webinar provides a platform for that. You can use a combination of Zoom and a simple PowerPoint to deliver training to a wide range of users en-masse, without heavy resources. If your timeline is short, and your budget is small, consider webinars.

Identifying the Correct Format for Your Education

At this point, you might be wondering how to ascertain which format is the best one for you from all the options we've provided above! It depends on a number of criteria, but let's break it down by three important considerations, with sub-questions you can consider for each one.

The Project

Here, you'll look at considerations that relate to the project itself.

How Long Do You Have to Develop Your Project?   This single question may immediately provide the answer you're looking for. If you only have a few weeks at your disposal, you won't be able to create an eLearning course or any blended learning experience. Focus on VILT or microlearning that requires much less production time. If you have more time, you have more options.

How Many People Do You Have on Your Team?   As above, if your resources are limited, VILT or microlearning is probably the way to go.

How Experienced Is Your Team?   Without sophisticated digital learning skills, we would advise caution before looking to develop a robust learning path. For minimal experience, lean on microlearning or VILT; for more experience, a self-paced course is on the table. Fully fledged learning paths should be reserved for those with a lot of experience.

Do You Need to Localize the Content?   If the learning needs to be translated into other languages, you want to keep things as simple as possible. A single course, one VILT, or microlearning is going to be your best route to limiting complexity.

The Audience

Now, think about the audience itself, who you're creating content for.

Is This Experience for One Learning Persona or Multiple?   With a single learning persona, you can take your pick from the types of content we've discussed. However, when you have to address multiple personas, you're adding complexity and need to factor in divergence. If you're targeting multiple learning personas, a blended course could be a good fit, where you can provide self-paced courses on common areas and then introduce inflection points where the education can diverge, handling that with ILT. Another option is to rely on ILT alone, rapidly iterating the content to suit the persona.

How Much Knowledge Does Your Audience Have?　If you're addressing an audience with no knowledge on the topic, microlearning or a self-paced course is best – something that covers the basics. It doesn't make sense to introduce ILT for foundational topics that every persona needs to know. It's not the best use of resources when this can be handled by self-instruction. If your learners have knowledge to build on, you'll need opportunities to modulate your training based on what they know, so blended learning or VILT becomes important. At the other end of the scale, if your learners have mastery already, an adaptive learning path can accommodate for that, surfacing relevant courses based on learner experience or levels of learning.

How Motivated Are Your Learners?　You may want to choose blended learning or VILT to make a course more interactive or to get some peer exchange or social learning involved. Self-paced courses are more effective if your learners are already excited or motivated to learn.

How Technically Proficient Are They?　If your audience isn't tech-savvy, then you're asking a lot of them to do an advanced self-paced course. It may be easier to offer them a video library or a Zoom training session.

What Is the Size of Your Audience?　If you are training more than one person at a time, you'll also need ILT. However, when the size of your audience gets much larger, you might want to offer some kind of blended learning where a large part of the education is self-paced, allowing the learning to be more hands-on. It's really hard to offer engaging ILT to a large audience, so if you're using this route, consider making it blended learning by offering breakout sessions or hands-on elements.

The Product

Now, turn your thoughts to your product. What exactly are you teaching your learners to do?

What Do You Need Learners to Know?　If the goal is for learners to have a small amount of knowledge, microlearning or a single course with one learning objective works best. If they need some level of mastery, then a blended course or a learning path is a better fit.

How Complex Is Your Product?   The more complex the product, the more support your audience will need. You're also likely to have more learning objectives, so you'll need to structure the education as multiple courses attached to an overarching goal within a learning path.

Bill Horzempa is the global manager of Education Services at Hewlett-Packard Enterprise. He speaks below about how to support the digital learner with the optimal learning experiences by choosing the right format for education.

Thoughts from . . . Bill Horzempa, Global Manager, Educational Services Global Delivery at Hewlett-Packard Enterprise

When we're thinking about the optimal delivery format for education at HPE, we always start by considering who our customers are and what they need. This manifests in a few different ways. For example, before the COVID-19 pandemic, globally we were split pretty evenly between instructor-led training (ILT) and virtual instructor-led training (VILT), with some cultures having more of an affinity with virtual classes than others. In the United States, we have found that customers readily accept VILT, and therefore there was little impact on course delivery during the pandemic. In other countries – such as Japan or Italy – it can take a little more encouragement to move to VILT, as they have more of a culture to learn physically on-site.

There might also be additional localization requirements that dictate the format – for example, customers who come from France or Russia regularly want their training in their native language, and are less likely to have as much confidence in English as a second language. We'll ask ourselves, "Is there value in localizing this content for different audiences?" If it's base-level, introductory content, and likely to get a lot of traction from a large number of learners, then an eLearning course localized to that language could be the right choice. However, if the content is quite niche, or we're expecting the customers to have questions, or the training to be more interactive, it

(continued)

makes sense to focus on instructor-led training where we can hire an instructor with proficiency in that language. The instructor can then take the materials and adapt their lecture to suit.

Our intent is always to provide knowledge in an optimal way for the customer. One delivery methodology we've had a lot of success with is hybrid, which allows us to offer the same class simultaneously in-person and also via VILT, which gives us a much larger ability to scale. Of course, for this hybrid format to work, you need a deeply skilled instructor who is able to handle both audiences and their differing needs.

In some cases, you might find that the audience dictates the format you choose. One of our instructors shared her story of a hybrid class she was running where 6 students were learning on-site, and 6 were leveraging the VILT training. On day 2, she set up the classroom, only to find that no one showed up in person. Logging into the VILT class, all 12 of the participants had opted for virtual learning! They hadn't seen any advantage to fighting the traffic and being there in person. To get this kind of reaction, your VILT experience needs to be very hands-on, available, and immersive. We work hard to ensure that short of physically touching the equipment, we're offering the same environment, and that we include virtual remote guidance so that the students can see the equipment live, both when they are conducting the lab work and when an instructor is showing how to replace components. This helps provide a similar experience to the face-to-face environment. When you're considering your format, think about how robust your technology is and what experience you can provide. Without the right infrastructure technology, you may need to fall back to onsite face-to-face delivery.

Supporting the Digital Learner with Blended Learning Opportunities

While our primary method of customer education is VILT/ILT, we're growing dramatically into supporting and encouraging the digital learner, with a learning-as-a-service methodology. As well as mirroring instructor-led training with the help of hands-on labs, we also offer eLearning and self-paced learning. Two excellent uses of this format are for prep classes so that everyone enters the ILT/VILT at the same level and for students to go back over material at the end of the class. Another self-paced learning format that's very powerful is lab sandbox environments, allowing customers to test and play in a safe, isolated space in their own time, outside of the classroom. This can be a good choice for something more technical where you really need that hands-on element, and where customers will get a lot of value out of practicing.

Every company is different, and each customer is different. We don't want to say, "Everyone will be able to take this course virtually and get what they need," because we know that won't suit all learners. With this in mind, to augment these self-paced offerings, we have enabled office hours, where if customers have signed up for a subscription, they can take advantage of getting personalized support and asking their questions to an expert. We also have a segment where we bring in an SME for a one-hour or two-hour mini class where they can provide an overview into a very focused topic. The point is that with a purely online course, you don't get the ability to speak to the instructor and clarify elements of your learning, so we want to offset that how we can.

Another consideration is how familiar the customers are with the product already, and where they are in terms of their maturity. Let's say HPE updates a line of servers. Our focus is making sure that customers can use the updates with maximum effectiveness. It's natural for us to develop a three- to five-day lecture lab class, developed and taught by an instructor using an ILT/VILT format. However, in this case, the base product may have already been out for several years and so many customers won't necessarily need to learn about the product from scratch. To solve this, we build "Delta" content and reach out by email or via a notification and say, "You took X class two years ago, we've added Y to the product, and we're offering this

(continued)

self-paced learning module to keep you up to date." Customers with one of our Digital Learner subscriptions can immediately log in and learn about the new features and how to implement them.

It's also essential to take time to consider the profit and loss element of the education you're creating before you pick a format, and consider whether something less formal will get the job done. If the product team approaches you with a very strategic product that they want a course for, it might be targeted at just 50 people worldwide and you may need to make a tough call that the financial investment in education just isn't worth it. In this case, it might make more sense to offer small-group informal sessions with engineers, rather than to create a whole ILT course for something relatively niche.

In general, when you're choosing a methodology or a format, it can help to ask yourself these questions:

- What knowledge does the customer need to know? Is this introductory content, or will it go deeper?
- Will your customers be able to pick up the information alone? And if not, do you have an SME or an instructor that is proficient to give this training?
- Can you offer a hybrid environment to allow for scalability and customer preferences?
- How does this impact profit/loss? What is the break-even point in terms of the number of students you need?

Choosing the right content format starts with going back to your initial goals for the education, and then thinking about your learners and what will prompt the best learning environment for their needs. Once you've decided on a format, it's time to consider exactly what content you need to include in the education.

8

Step 6: Make Content Engaging and Efficient for the Busy Customer

After you've identified the optimal format for educating the customer at the relevant point in their lifecycle, it's time to turn your mind to content itself and determine what you need to include. This can be a really fun and immersive step, where you can get in front of a whiteboard and start thinking about all the different things that you want your customers to learn and how to link content to specific learning objectives.

Start by defining these learning objectives. A lot of people skip this step, feeling that it's laborious or that it won't be helpful, but if you feel tempted to breeze past this – don't! At the end of the day, when you write down your learning objectives, you get a lot of clarity about what needs to be included in your education and what doesn't. With a learning objective in place, you can narrow down what content you include to be anything that aligns to the learning objective, and nothing that doesn't, knowing that ultimately anything that doesn't align will detract from the lesson. This makes the whole process a lot smoother and more accurate. Learning objectives also make it easier to see at a glance if you're trying to achieve too much with a single course or training session.

Creating Learning Objectives

One great method for creating learning objectives is to use Bloom's Taxonomy to classify the levels of learning that take place (see Figure 8.1). Bloom's is usually symbolized with some form of pyramid, where verbs related to the lowest levels of learning are written at the bottom and deeper learning activities are covered as you move your way up toward the apex.

Learning objectives use these verbs to explain what the customer is going to learn. The basic verbs start with *remember, understand,* and *apply* before getting deeper to *analyze, evaluate,* and finally *create*.

To obtain the highest level of learning, where your customers can really take deeper meaning from your education and apply it to novel situations or truly evaluate and analyze what they've been taught, your learners need to start with the foundational level of learning.

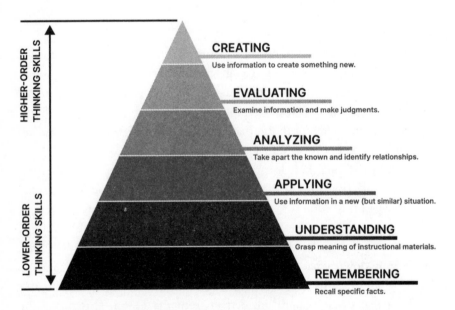

Figure 8.1 Bloom's Taxonomy

Simply put, before you can apply learning, you need to understand it. Before you can evaluate, you need to analyze. This means that your course needs to build on prior knowledge.

Bloom's Taxonomy is a great way to ensure that learning objectives follow this path. For example, start with, "*Memorize* the definition of these three new words" and "*Explain* the meaning of these words" before asking the learner to "*Demonstrate* the ability to use them in a new context" or to "*Evaluate* the impact of their usage."

In SaaS terms, your early learning objectives could be as simple as committing something to memory, such as where to click to get started, while by the end of the course, you may want your learner to be able to create something from scratch using your software. You need the foundational steps to get to the ultimate learning outcome. We've found that using Bloom's Taxonomy forces you to think about the order of learning and create learning objectives that map this journey in a smart way.

While each course may have a dozen lessons, best practice is that each should have a single learning objective to allow you to really focus in on what the customer is learning. There may also be a course-level objective – an overall learning goal for the whole course or learning path – but each lesson works best with a single learning objective that moves your learner sequentially higher up the pyramid.

Personalizing Objectives for Personas

If you've done the foundational work of creating learning personas and identifying what each of these customers needs to know to achieve success, you should be able to take your learning objectives and identify for each persona what their objectives should be at each stage. It could be that some are the same across your personas, but perhaps there are a few deviations somewhere along the learning path. Your admin users might need learning at a deeper level than non-admin users, for example. Now's the time to identify the inflection points where you want to do something different with your education.

You may have the ability to set up content provisioning, where you can customize your courses automatically for specific audiences. At Thought Industries, we have a feature called Panorama that allows you to provision content for your customers based on their needs, so that when they log in to your education, they see a dedicated customer learning channel for them – branded, customized, and unique to their needs. This is especially helpful if you have customers who use your product in a really unique way. If you don't have the means to provision content in this way, you can still set up different learning paths and ask your users to self-select.

Auditing and Categorizing Content

Now that you've created your learning objectives and assigned certain learning personas as necessary, you can start bringing content to the conversation. When you create education, it shouldn't be a matter of always starting from square one. If you're going to be successful at scaling your team and meeting the demands of the business, you need to think about how to leverage existing content.

If you haven't already, conduct an audit that categorizes your existing content by topic and aligns each asset to at least one learning objective, as seen in Figure 8.2. With this audit in place, you can now address your content creation like a puzzle. You have your personas, and you have each learning objective next to its relevant persona. Now, you can begin bringing in existing content that can be associated with that learning objective. What already exists and can be repurposed? What exists in one format, but needs to be adapted or modified? Where are there gaps? What you should begin to see as you fill in this puzzle is a sequential path through your lessons (each with their own learning objective) that leads to a greater learning outcome. As your learning path is coming together, you should start identifying what you need to put effort into, whether that's transforming existing content or creating new content from a blank page.

At Thought Industries, we host a weekly VILT series called Office Hours, an hour-long session where we deep-dive into a single feature or how to do a specific task or action using our platform. After a year, we had collected more than 50 hours of content from these webinars. It's not realistic or even helpful to expect customers to watch these in full, so we took the video content that we had accumulated, sliced and diced it into smaller microlearnings focused on specific topics, and then categorized it based on what each piece of content can teach. We now have hundreds of pieces of content, and as we're categorizing courses, we can pull them in on-demand.

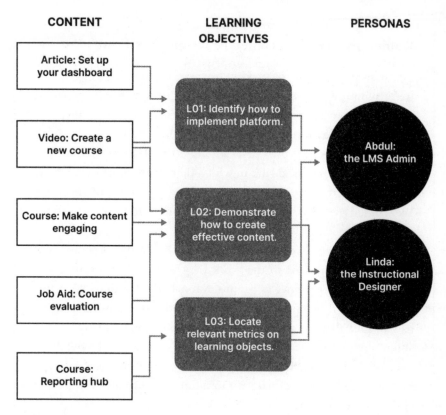

Figure 8.2 Aligning Content to Learners

Merrill's First Principles of Instruction

David Merrill is the author of the *First Principles of Instruction,* an instructional theory shown in Figure 8.3 that we like to use when considering exactly what content to include in customer education. Merrill includes a foundational idea in his Principles of Instruction: "Information is not Education."[1] A learning experience is so much more than just lifting knowledge from the mind of the teacher to the mind of the student; the proverbial *tabula rasa* to be scribbled on.

Merrill's first principle is problem-centered. He puts forward that – for learning to be at its most effective, engaging, and efficient – learners need a problem-centered strategy that involves real-world, relatable tasks.

---

[1] David Merrill, *First Principles of Instruction* (Hoboken, NJ: John Wiley & Sons, 2012).

Daniel on the Importance of Keeping It Real

Often, in the interests of making learning more engaging and fun, we're tempted to create a fantastic story or a whole new world around what we're teaching. I remember that I was once involved in designing a learning experience around how people could coach their employees. In our first attempt, the learner became an adventurer in a mythical land in which there were quirky characters who came across problems as they moved through the coaching. We named it "Vivian Vance and the Quest for the Crown of Coaching"!

The feedback we received was that people didn't understand how it was connected to the work they were doing – some even described the experience as "unprofessional," the last thing you want to hear when developing professional training. Similarly, at Asana we had an idea that we called "Mission to the Moon." As you learned about how to use the project management software, you would hire your pilot, fuel your spaceship, and discover an outer-space adventure. We were trying to make it more fun and engaging, but people said, "I'm not an astronaut!"

While these felt like good ideas to me at the time, learning can be promoted more effectively by using real-world tasks and scenarios. This means that there is no abstraction necessary to figure out how to apply the lesson; it becomes obvious. The learner approaches it and immediately can recognize a problem that they are facing every day.

Merrill's second principle of promoting learning is to activate any prior knowledge that the customer already has, to access and awaken the mental model around the topic so you can build on that foundation. Think about what you've already taught the customer or what they've picked up on their own, and reiterate those examples to tap into a previous experience.

The third principle is demonstration. Once you choose what you want to include, you will need to incorporate content that demonstrates the skill, anything from a live instruction or video content to a screen grab or even a GIF to show the learner how the information is applied.

LEARNING IS PROMOTED WHEN:

Problem-Centered	01	Learners are engaged in solving real-world problems.
Activation	02	Existing knowledge is activated as a foundation for new knowledge.
Demonstration	03	New knowledge is demonstrated to the learner.
Application	04	New knowledge is applied by the learner.
Integration	05	New knowledge is integrated into the learner's world.

Figure 8.3 Merrill's Principles of Instruction

Merrill's fourth principle is application. A lot of times in customer education, tests are used that aim for the lowest level of Bloom's Taxonomy, merely expecting the learner to remember or parrot back information. We then consider this a signal that learning has taken place. However, when you're in a job, recalling a fact isn't enough. Instead, learners need to apply a skill or knowledge in a novel situation when they need to tackle a problem. That's why the most effective learning experiences are those that require learners to apply their knowledge like they would in a real-world scenario.

For application, simulations are good, but as we said earlier – they are usually expensive. Instead, try a scenario-based assessment. Set up a story or a case study and ask your learners what they would do in a specific situation. At Optimizely, we had an assessment called "Which One Won?" where we gave learners two variations of a website. They had completed training on experimentation strategy and A/B testing, and we asked them to decide which variation was the winner, with extra credit if they could explain why. This was a great way for them to apply their newfound knowledge.

Merrill's fifth principles is integration. At the activation stage, we asked learners to recall their existing mental model so that they could build on it and add new skills. At this stage, those skills are integrated. For this to happen, we ask learners to engage, to reflect on what they've learned, and to share it with someone else through activities such as peer collaboration and peer critique. With this level of reflection, you're taking learning to a deeper processing level and allowing customers to make the cognitive leap from learning into something actionable that they can integrate into how they do their job. Examples include asking learners to reflect on what they've learned and name something that was useful or helpful or offering a message board or a forum where learners can debate what they've taken in.

Introducing Gagné's Nine Events of Instruction

Robert Gagné is an educational psychologist who pioneered the science of instruction in the 1940s. He created a hierarchy of learning called "Nine Events of Instruction," shown in Figure 8.4,[2] that describes the elements required for effective learning. This model has become a common framework for educators when they're designing instruction so that it's engaging and optimized for learning.

Daniel on Gagné versus Merrill

There are a lot of similarities between Gagné's Nine Events and Merrill's Principles of Instruction, but if I had to compare them, I would say that Gagné's model works best for classroom instruction, while Merrill's works for any kind of learning experience. Gagné's was the framework I knew first, and I love the sequential nature of the levels; it's a real blueprint for the learning experience, allowing you to drop content into each level to work out exactly what you need to include. When I then came across Merrill's Principles of Instruction, though, I was drawn to its focus on problem-centered learning, which feels particularly relevant for customer education. However, I lean on both when I'm thinking about what content to include in my learning journeys.

Event 1: Grab the Attention of Your Learner. Everyone has been part of the classroom experience where the teacher starts talking and everyone zones out. The first interaction with the learner is really important

---

[2] R. M. Gagné, L. J. Briggs, and W. W. Wager, "The Events of Instruction," in R. M. Gagné, L. J. Briggs, and W. W. Wager (eds.) *Principles of Instructional Design* (4th ed.) (Fort Worth, TX: Harcourt Brace College Publishers, 1992).

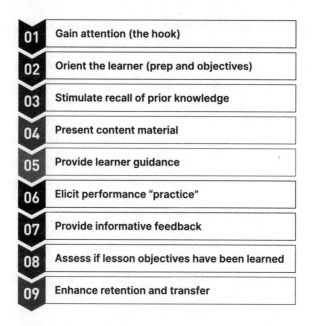

Figure 8.4 Gagné's Nine Events

because it grabs them by the shoulders and says, "Listen up! This is worth your time!" There are so many ways to do this, including starting with a joke or an anecdote, incorporating an icebreaker, or bringing out a related prop as a conversation starter.

Event 2: Inform the Learner of Your Objectives.   This is as simple as saying, "Today, you're going to learn about XYZ." Not only have you bought the learner into why they should be paying attention, signaling to what you'll be learning has the dual effect of priming the pump; getting the listeners to start thinking about the topic ahead of time.

Event 3: Simulate the Recall of Previous Knowledge.   Simulating recall is similar to Merrill's second principle in the previous framework. You bring to the surface the mental model for what you're about to teach. Think about any earlier learning, either formal or informal, and then think how it dovetails into what you're going to learn. Ask questions here like "How many people have been in a training experience on this topic before?" "Was it positive or negative, and why?" Encourage them to retrieve what they've learned.

Event 4: Present the New Information.   At this point, you'll begin to provide the learning content itself. The mental model has been primed, you're ready to teach. Make sure to organize this information in a logical way, and mix it up with different media and modalities to keep the lesson engaging and stimulating for all different kinds of learners.

Event 5: Provide Guidance for the Learner.   Examples help to create better learning outcomes. Add case studies, stories, or analogies, and mark places to ask your learners to do the same, contributing with examples that help them to understand what they're being taught. Take time to help your learners retain the information by guiding them through how it applies in the real world.

Event 6: Ask Learners to Practice and Perform.   Now's the point to make sure that you've included content that helps people to demonstrate what they've learned. This isn't where you test your learners; you're not ready for a summative exam here. Instead, think about role-play exercises or practice with the product.

Event 7: Reinforce and Provide Feedback.   Hand-in-hand with the previous event, you're then able to provide feedback to users in the moment. Imagine the example of an art class, where you ask learners to practice by sketching a still life drawing. This isn't their final exam; it's just practice. As the instructor, you can then walk around the room and provide feedback and guidance to reinforce what the artists have learned in class.

Event 8: Assess to See if Learning Took Place.   I've heard some debate on whether assessments and tests have a place in customer education. If you're going to offer a certificate of completion or any kind of badging, you definitely need a strong signal that learning has taken place. A signal will help the learner, of course, but it also helps you as a business to recognize what your customers know.

Event 9: Enhance Retention and Transfer.   Make sure to have a plan in place for the forgetting curve. Once the learner has completed the course, what are you going to do to enhance their levels of retention? Will you have a follow-up session? How will you reinforce what they have learned to consolidate the knowledge?

Don't forget to go back to our trifecta of time, scope, and budget while you're planning your content. It can be easy to get carried away, but it's important to verify that the content you choose can be obtained from your budget. Often, the reality might run up against your dream, but don't let perfection become the enemy of your progress – stay true to the goals for your education within the means at your disposal.

Making Learning Efficient, Effective, and Engaging

Content is never just content. You can create the best educational materials out there and check off every stage of any particular framework, and it means very little if you can't get your learners to engage and retain. In the journal *Educational Technology,* Merrill suggests a rubric for considering his First Principles of Instruction.[3] He calls this "Finding e3" (effective, efficient, and engaging instruction).

As you create your learning experience, you may find that any one of these rises or falls as you tweak the others. It can be somewhat of a balancing act! Let's start with efficient. When we think about making learning efficient, we have to acknowledge that our customers are busy people. They have their own jobs to do that don't involve learning about your product. They may recognize the value in learning what you have to offer, but they want to get it done as quickly as possible. Ask yourself: Have you created an experience that is as simple and as concise as possible to get the learning across? If something isn't relevant, then it's filler.

However, if we accept that as a fact, we run into problems when we start building content for the next e – engaging. Sometimes, in an effort to create a learning experience that is efficient and relevant, we forget to provide ways to engage the learner with the experience. The goal is to get the learner into the 'flow' state, where they are highly tuned into the present and far more receptive to what they are learning. But if anything that's not relevant is filler, then any engaging element needs to serve a learning purpose, or it's not an efficient use of people's time.

When you have found a way to create efficient learning experiences without losing the emphasis on engagement, it can be helpful to focus on

---

[3] David Merrill, "Finding e3 (Effective, Efficient, and Engaging) Instruction," *Educational Technology* 49, no. 3 (May–June 2009): 15–26.

one final e – effective – as quality assurance. Is this the most effective way that you can present this content to the learner? Ask yourself why you think it is, and then ask yourself again! Is this the simplest route to your intended outcome? Does it facilitate that state of flow? Will it keep learners interested?

Sometimes you may find that, when you put on your learning science hat and you're working on making the content as engaging, effective, and efficient as you can, you have to let go of strictly adhering to a framework to get the results that you need.

Daniel on Creating Focused Content

I once had an interesting moment when I was presenting to an audience of my peers how I designed a customer education course for Optimizely. I described how I was going to use a precourse quiz to activate the learner the way that Merrill describes in his principles and stimulate recall the way that Gagné outlines in his levels. This would be a short quiz so that people could think about what they already knew and also prime themselves for what was coming next. A colleague of mine, Alessandra Marinetti, was in the audience, and she asked me if I had thought about how it might cause people who didn't want to take a test to drop out early. We went ahead with that format and found that she was absolutely right – the test was having a negative impact on course completion rates, which was what we really needed to achieve.

I always think about this example when I consider eliminating elements of the learning experience. Scientifically, there may have been benefits to the test, but ultimately, I needed busy professionals to be engaged with what I was providing. Today, that's become core to my strategy for customer education: remembering that every minute customers spend on learning is one minute less that they have in their day to do their jobs. That's informed a lot of the focused, short, and modular microlearning-style content that I champion.

Leave Space for Rabbit Trails!

We've talked a lot about creating focused content based on specific learning objectives, but it's also important to allow space for discovery for those customers who want more information. Think about what you feel your customers "must know" versus what is "nice to know." The nice-to-know content might not be suitable for a focused lesson, but can be used as a way for customers to go deeper into the topic. These resources can be listed at the end of the course for further reading, for example.

Some kinds of learning are more likely to attract customer questions. If the format of your education is live training, you're definitely going to want to take some time to anticipate what questions your audience may have and create a plan for answering these. This could be offering Frequently Asked Questions (FAQs) for the topic or gathering additional content together that's related to a "nice to know" ahead of time. These rabbit trails allow for more depth and exploration for those who want it.

Considering introductory or additional learning materials will be especially important if you're introducing a new concept or type of product to the market. Head of customer education at Miro, Dee Kapila shares her thoughts on what it means to create customer education for a "category-defining product."

Thoughts from . . . Dee Kapila, Head of Customer Education, Miro

One of Miro's core organizational values is to continuously practice empathy to gain insight, and so our team's process is to first talk to learners to understand their context, then research the core problem they need to solve, before pinpointing an approach that will best benefit them. Ideally, we want to decrease friction and help learners get value from our product in 90 seconds or less. To do this effectively, we keep the learner and their problem at the forefront of our course discovery and research phase, but we keep coming back to the problem and the learner persona throughout the course development cycle.

(continued)

As an example, we recently released a course on designing and delivering workshops. Our persona was the workshop facilitator, so we did a lot of research to understand their challenges, outlined their core Jobs-to-be-Done (JTBD) statements, and then drafted learning outcomes to ensure that by the end of the course, they could accomplish the three big jobs they had helped us understand they wanted to do using Miro. These jobs were broken down into three phases: What do they need to do before a workshop? How will they facilitate great insights during the workshop? And how will they drive outcomes after a workshop? Understanding learner needs through the entire journey helped us to develop this multiphase course, checking all the boxes learners were looking for us to fill.

We don't stop there. Once the course has been released, we think about the learner's broader context. They may come to our academy to learn, but it's more likely that they'll want to access the learning in-product, or within their organization's LMS or LXP. So we create in-app learning and also distribute our content in a way that lets them pull it into their internal learning systems for consumption. You want to address the learning need end-to-end, and a course is just one part of that.

Minimizing Cognitive Load for the Learner

What's interesting at Miro specifically is that we're a category-defining product. If a customer is very familiar with Microsoft Word, then getting them into using Google Docs is conceptually more manageable – you're building on a vocabulary they already have by adding a cloud concept or a live editing concept. Miro is a visual whiteboard with an infinite canvas, and as this is something new in the market, it's more of a cognitive leap to understand. We have to address and streamline the conceptual leap for an infinite canvas whiteboard as well as the changes in fine motor skills, the spatial learning that's required to complete a task. Learning outcomes are really important in this case to help us hit both sides of that shift.

To help us design effective training, we developed our skillmap, which details core skills within the product and then allots points across the breadth and depth of that skill to account for cognitive complexity. By using Bloom's Taxonomy, we look at every feature inside our visual collaboration platform and, for each layer, add 1 to 6 points depending on if it is a lower-order or higher-order thinking skill. The skillmap and associated points help us design focused training that helps the learner achieve their goal while minimizing cognitive overload.

We never forget that our customers are the experts in what needs to be done. A lot of new learners aren't familiar with canvas tools, but that doesn't mean they aren't experts in their competency or use case in a different format. If we're getting our education right – we're coming in with practical tools that can help them to achieve their goals or co-create seamlessly in a new way that they think is an improvement on the status quo.

Optimizing Content for Retention

In terms of retention, we use a lot of stories and analogies to ground customers in multiple contextual situations where everyone has experience. So first, we might present the tool and show how it works, then we zoom out to show it in use across multiple contexts like strategic planning, facilitating a meeting, or leading an agile ceremony. Suddenly, these use cases have helped a feature come to life in the form of meaningful scenarios and storytelling.

Another way to boost retention is to focus on improving the experience for learners who, like me, aren't doing all of their learning at a desk. They're watching a few quick videos from their mobile phone in the morning before they're ready to start the day, or on their commute on the city bus. We want to make our education as easy as possible for learners to consume, so we create short videos that are all-inclusive and don't require you to pull in information

(continued)

from somewhere else, something that can quickly become a disjointed or a jarring experience. We optimize these with UI highlighting, tooltips and hot-key popups, and accessibility best practices, all of which provide context to what the viewer is seeing so they don't have to then supplement it with a job aid or something else to bring the key concepts together. We've found that talking heads work well to add warmth and break up a screencast, as do breaks and pauses with animation or music to really make the learning bite-sized and approachable within a single video. Depending on your culture and your brand, you might be able to infuse humor, which can also add engagement to the experience.

The Importance of Hands-On Activities

Our product is a visual collaboration product, in fact, our company's name was inspired by the iconoclastic artist Joan Miro. We believe that everyone is an artist and Miro is your canvas. It follows then, that all our learning includes moments for learners to flex their skills in a hands-on way. Our contextual education experience releases hands-on templates where users can Find it, See it, Try it – meaning, locate a feature, see it in action and then get hands-on themselves. Our courses all come with "exercise files" in the form of course Miro-boards, which follow the Lego play model, to help learners apply and retain core skills.

By the end of this stage, you should have decided what you want to include in your education, and what is unnecessary or can be offered as an optional "rabbit trail." You should also have some idea of how you're going to keep learners engaged and excited about what you have to teach! Your next focus will be the trainers themselves, nurturing relationships with instructors and SMEs, and ensuring that you stay up to date on the product roadmap.

9

Step 7: Who Trains the Trainers? Transforming Your Team into Experts

By now, you've determined what content to include in your education. You should also have a plan to ensure that it's effective for the customer, is created according to proven best-practices, and meets your overarching learning objectives. Now it's time to turn your head to who will be delivering the education. The success of your education depends heavily on people outside of your own team, so you'll need to consider how to choose the right instructors, which subject matter experts (SMEs) to speak with, and how to keep all stakeholders educated and aligned on the product roadmap.

Choosing Trainers for ILT

A common question people ask when hiring trainers for instructor-led training (ILT) is whether instructors need to be subject matter experts. Especially for a technical product, do they need to be technically proficient themselves, or should you lean toward those who are great trainers and not worry about a technical background or skillset?

When you're hiring a trainer, there's no doubt that you need to look for certain core competencies around training. These include the ability to facilitate conversation, to make thoughtful inquiries and quick decisions on the fly, and to recognize when customers understand what they're being taught and when they need more support.

When you're interviewing candidates, you'll see that some instructors may be expert trainers but have poor technical knowledge. Others may be technically skilled but have less experience in training itself. It can be difficult to find people who blend both skills, as instructors are often developers, product managers, or support agents who have a technical background and found that they enjoy training, which led to a career pivot.

There are great things about technically proficient trainers. These candidates will come to the table with a mastery of the subject area and easily understand technical concepts without needing you to do a lot of work. They will be able to build on their previous technical knowledge to identify smart ways to deliver technical training.

However, the risk of having someone in front of the classroom who doesn't have training experience is that they may struggle with translating that knowledge into easily digestible learning experiences. They might also have what we call *the curse of knowledge* – they know so much that they make assumptions about the learner's own foundational knowledge. The consequences of this are steep. If our assumptions are erroneous, we end up pitching the education at the wrong level, overcomplicating something that's relatively simple, or overwhelming the learner.

On the flip side, you are also likely to speak to candidates who have little technical background but who are expert trainers. They may have a background in instructional design or innate knowledge on how to support learning transference. They will be experienced in engaging learners, managing the classroom effectively and making decisions intuitively and quickly according to learner needs, such as when to spend more time on a given topic or when the audience is getting overwhelmed with information. However, they're not an SME. If they can't answer questions about the technical aspects of the product, this can undermine the learning process and compromise your credibility. It's common for trainers who are not proficient in the subject matter to provide incorrect or misleading information, which can cause irreparable harm.

So, does the trainer need to be an SME? We've spoken about the 80/20 rule already, how 80 percent of what your customers need to do is covered by 20 percent of what you could teach them. In our opinion, your trainer needs to be an expert on that 20 percent, the foundational content. Even if they are the most enthusiastic instructor, if trainers simply read a script without having fluency over that 20 percent, they will lose credibility the moment someone asks a question. For anything outside of that 20 percent, the trainer should have a breadth of knowledge around additional resources so they can act as a concierge to appropriately connect learners with the information that they need.

Whichever balance you find in training versus technical expertise, one thing is critical: Your trainers must have absolute subject matter mastery in the area of value proposition. They need to know back to front how the product is going to help customers to achieve success and be able to communicate that to learners clearly and thoroughly. Having a basic knowledge of the technicalities is fine, but the most important thing is to ensure that trainers can explain how the product will help customers to meet their own goals.

Working with SMEs

You've chosen your trainers. How will you ensure that they develop and deepen their knowledge? The primary way to establish fluency with a technical topic is to conduct expert interviews with SMEs. Building relationships with stakeholders and conducting this kind of discovery interview is really important for both instructor-led training and eLearning.

Nurture Relationships with SMEs

As soon as you arrive at a new company, you should start thinking about your relationships with SMEs. Don't wait until you need them for a specific project. Make sure that you've introduced yourself, make them feel special, let them know that they are going to play an important role in your work. Explain that you're relying on their beautiful and complex knowledge so that you can create learning experiences that help the customer and the business. We've seen many times throughout our careers that with nurtured partnerships in place, customer education professionals can tap into knowledge far easier when the time comes, getting quick input from an SME and allowing you to scale and go-to-market faster. Of course, make sure that you make it clear you won't be overwhelming them with asks – that you're cognizant of their workload and respectful of their time.

Once you're meeting with an SME for a specific task or project, always start by explaining the goal. Make sure that they know what the content will accomplish and how it aligns to the business goals. For example, if a customer education stakeholder was going to speak to an SME at Thought Industries about how to create custom dashboards using the Reporting Hub (a robust analytics feature), they shouldn't just ask, "How does the Reporting Hub work?" Instead, they could say, "The goal of these articles is to help customers create custom dashboards. This is important because it helps customers manipulate data to see the value of the work that they do. They can then communicate it to their own stakeholders, which means greater engagement and more upsell opportunities for us." Start at the beginning and explain why it's important for both the customer and the business. Now your SME is plugged into why the education matters.

Before your interview, prepare questions that you will ask the SME. These could include:

> *"How is this topic going to help your customers to achieve success?"*
> *"What job does this help the customers do?"*
> *"What other features is it connected to?"*
> *"Why should customers care about this?"*
> *"What must customers know (20 percent), and what is it nice to know (80 percent)?"*
> *"In a world where customers are using this optimally – what does that look like?"*

Once you have these answers, you should be getting an idea of why this feature is valuable and how it's connected to the overall product experience.

Your next step is to address friction. You might find that some SMEs were deeply involved in product or design and therefore find it hard to consider that there could be pain points involved, but this is an important step in your interview. Ask the SME to reflect on where the customer might struggle, or what foundational knowledge they expect the user to have to use the product optimally. In the example of the Reporting Hub, it could be that users need some fluency with data fields or visualization, and with the SMEs guidance, you could proactively support these users with education rather than resorting to reacting to support tickets.

In some situations, you might be conducting a group session with multiple SMEs. If that's the case, leverage tools like whiteboards, sticky notes, or other strategies that can help you organize your discussion. Think about how you're going to facilitate discovery in a way that prompts quieter people to get involved and provide input. For example, you might write questions on different areas of a whiteboard and ask SMEs to post sticky notes that capture their thoughts.

Be Clear on Expectations

Don't forget to share the work you did in Step 4, when you created your customer education development plan. Make sure that you've reiterated the SMEs involvement according to the RASCI model you've created, and describe the scope and timeline of the project. You might want to ask for supporting materials such as product design documents or marketing information to augment the overall story you're creating. You may have specific questions that this stakeholder isn't best equipped to answer and will need someone else who can help you fill in the blanks. Whatever your needs, if you have explicit expectations of the SME – such as making an introduction, writing an article or providing data – be clear and make sure you have mutual agreement, or you could end up with misaligned expectations.

Recognize and Reward Your SME's Work

Once you've completed the interview, thank your SME, and reiterate how important their contribution is to your process, making sure to indicate that you'll follow up. It's important to update them on your status and to recognize their input. At Optimizely, Adam Avramescu was fond of saying,

"We are all educators." Every time he stood up to talk about customer education, he would reiterate how everyone across the company was an educator, whether they were in customer success, or sales, or they put a label into a tool or a product – everyone is an educator in some small way. When someone would formally contribute to customer education, like in an SME interview, they would earn a T-shirt that had "We are all educators" printed as a slogan! However you choose to approach this, it is important to express gratitude and make your SMEs and contributors feel special. You may even want to provide a mechanism for mutual feedback, helping you to be more effective in your research, and providing a standardized route for you to show appreciation.

Educate the Team on the Product Roadmap

Of course, it's not scalable to sit down with an SME every time your product changes. If you work in a software company, you may have a release every two weeks. You'll only speak to an SME when you're developing a relatively deep learning experience. Educational materials are a critical part of the assets that need to be developed for a product launch, alongside product marketing, messaging, sales enablement, and support for customer success. However, so many companies don't include customer education in the conversation until it's too late to make this happen with impact.

You will therefore need to establish a person from your team who will be responsible for aligning with the product roadmap – the GTM strategy of the company. This person ensures that everyone is updated on the changing nature of the product in what is often a dynamic and fast-paced environment. When we discussed the trifecta of time, scope, and budget, you may remember touching on the idea that your timeline may not always be within your own hands. It's important to keep customer education stakeholders in the loop, as there is often a very small window between when the product or feature update is ready and when it's being launched.

It's essential to ensure that your team is educated on the changing face of the product. Often, the changes are small – a minor tweak to something that already exists, or a modification to the way that a feature is used. However, even small changes can have a big impact on your education, such as the need to change a screenshot in a help-desk article if the dashboard has been updated or to amend a tutorial if navigation buttons have moved.

In the absence of a process for including customer education stakeholders in the GTM strategy, your team might not be aware of a new feature until it's already in QA and about to go live, or in a worst-case scenario, until after it's gone live. As an education team, then, you're left scrambling to create documentation and a learning experience that will allow your customer to gain value on launch day.

So, how do you go about getting included in the continuous GTM roadmap?

First, make it clear to the product and marketing teams that education is an important part of being ready for every release. At first, they might see this as a delay, another stakeholder to include in the conversation. Explain the pain as well as the consequences for the customer and the business of not having educational materials on launch day – not even a single knowledge base article to explain some background or to help with friction.

Before the GTM process was born, marketing and sales also had this challenge. A product feature might get developed and released, but marketing and sales teams weren't sure how to sell it. But now, in a mature company, product marketing managers and sales managers ensure that there is a strategy in place to have the relevant assets in place for launch day. Explain that this is exactly where you need to insert a customer education stakeholder!

It could be setting up an auto-include or auto-assign on a particular board in your project management tool, or it might be a physical meeting that you need to make sure appears on the right stakeholder's calendar.

At Asana, every time there was a new product release, a project was spun up according to a template. The template included all the tasks that needed to be accomplished to go live with the feature. The relevant assignees were alerted when the project was opened, and each stakeholder could mark when elements were complete. Everything was centralized in a single project, and so everyone had access to all the documentation and information. This made it extremely easy to prepare for launch.

Not everyone uses collaboration software, but whatever the process at your organization, there is likely to be a GTM team that meets on a regular cadence to make sure that there is a plan in place for upcoming product changes and releases. You need to make sure that you've raised your hand – this is an important conversation for you to be involved in! Joining the "GTM Release" team will provide you with the advance notice that you need to be able to plan ahead for education, whether that's taking screenshots, adjusting or creating tutorials, creating help-desk articles, or anything else.

The Role of Customer Education in Learning Enablement

If we accept that "we are all educators" and that customers are always learning, whether the customer comes into contact with your organization from a chat with a sales rep, through their QBR with a CSM, or when they read a blog created by the marketing team, then it stands to reason that customer education has an important role in educating these educators!

There's no doubt that the organization works more cohesively when everyone is aligned with the same learning goals and understands the problems that customers want to solve, as well as how your product helps them to achieve that. Training professionals often have broad skills in instructional design, learning science, and storytelling. They also know a great deal about the product and usually have hands-on experience teaching new customers how to master it. Perhaps more than any other professional, they are equipped to develop and deliver learning experiences that nurture customers from prospects to advocates. By working together with other teams across the organization, training specialists can drive powerful results across the entire customer lifecycle.

We spoke back in Chapter 2 about how we structure the customer education team at Thought Industries, under the department of Learning Strategies. Let's go into that structure in more detail, with how it impacts the goal of learning enablement in mind. If you recall, Learning Strategies has the charter of "Educate the market, educate the customer, and educate the team." It has three distinct functions:

1. **Industry research.** Focus on best-practices through a center of excellence around the critical challenges that customer education stakeholders face. This research is used to publish our own content, and also help create awareness of our brand, drive discourse, and solve problems in the community.

2. **Customer education.** Help customers to realize value, and leverage the product to achieve success. This is accomplished not only through product training, but also through enabling our customers to achieve success in their roles. Our industry research plays a big role in our own customer education strategy, and we strive to "drink our own champagne" by modeling best practices.

3. **Internal training.** Enable our own team to feel confident around the product, engage with learning materials, and achieve greater fluency with the challenges that our customers face. In other words, we teach our own team to speak the language of our customers, which helps them gain credibility, generates more enthusiasm, nurtures more empathy, and develops more confidence – ultimately becoming better educators themselves.

Here are a few examples of functions that customer education can support in any organization.

Sales

Customer education should work closely with sales enablement to help sales reps better present the product, demo it in a way that's aligned to the learning needs of prospects, and better overcome objections to close more deals faster. Customer education can offer content and knowledge around how the product works, problems customers commonly hope to solve, and expertise around designing demos and presentations in a way that is engaging and optimized for learning. As a result, sales reps will be able to present to prospects in a way that wins trust, establishes trust, and promotes behavioral change (in this case, conversions!).

Customer Support

Depending on the technical proficiency of your customer education team, you can help to teach support reps technical aspects of the product as well as how to answer FAQs. Customer education can also highlight elements of the product customers may struggle with and provide solutions optimized for learning. Finally, and perhaps most importantly, customer education can enable customer support on the documentation and job aids to use in order to resolve customer friction.

Marketing

Customer education can work with marketing to uncover customer value and align with new updates and features to create effective content that educates as well as sells. Additionally, because customer education teams are often deeply immersed in customer value and industry best-practices, they can play a big role in driving brand-building thought leadership. From blog articles to product release notes, customer education can help connect the product to the problems customers want to solve.

Human Resources

Customer education can provide new hires with a fundamental understanding of the product, its value, and why customers use it – helping them to get onboarded quicker. This will directly align their own introduction to the product with the learning needs of the customer. Moreover, it can foster a deeper sense of empathy with customers – a skill that's useful no matter the role.

While in many organizations, customer education, L&D, and sales enablement currently exist as siloed teams within their respective departments, we predict a convergence, as Learning Strategies can bring all of these together to work as a powerful whole.

Your Partner Training Program – Train the Trainer

Another example of educating the team who will deliver the education is a partner training program. This is a great way to scale the customer education team with community members, channel partners, and resellers or distributors who sell your product or service on your behalf. They may use on-demand training sessions or YouTube videos, create their own white-labeled academy using something like Thought Industries' Panorama, or they might offer an instructor-led training experience. As your education initiatives become more popular, you might explore a partner program as a strategy to scale the customer education function and introduce more prospects to your brand, and deepen engagement with your customers.

It's important to acknowledge that the goal of partner training isn't the same as for customer education. It's not always about driving product adoption, but rather, it's about enabling your partners to market, sell, and teach your product on your behalf. Partner training is foundational to a successful partner program, so let's discuss some best practices.

Create a Guide

This will be the manual that you give your partners – your train-the-trainer guide. It's great to use existing content, but this should be reformatted and curated into a partner training manual that allows your partners to understand the resources that they have at their disposal. Start with some kind of assessment, as your partners will have varying levels of expertise. Some might be experts and therefore insulted if you start with a course on the basics. Your goal here is the same as with hiring instructors. You need to ensure they are fluent in the 20 percent that makes up 80 percent of customer use cases, and also that they are super familiar with the value proposition. If your partners are selling, you will also need to include education around common objections, competitive differentiators, and product marketing messaging.

Consider a Certification Program

This can be a great option to standardize and enforce requirements among your partner base to prove a minimum level of expertise that allows them to speak on your behalf. This should be something that they need to stay up to date with and can show legitimacy through a badge or a qualification that they can put on their website or on LinkedIn. At Optimizely, we offered three layers: a basic partner certification that proved you could help customers set up, implement, and use Optimizely; a developer certification that showed you could customize the Optimizely platform on a technical level; and a strategy certification which meant you were skilled at identifying where, how, and why customers should implement experiments to their best advantage. We would direct customers to partners depending on how the customer's needs aligned with the partner's relative areas of expertise.

Continue to Educate Your Partners

You'll need a plan in place for how you keep partners up to date. You may want to offer a monthly webinar exclusive to partners or a shared workspace where you can offer current templates, file sharing, and brand guidelines, all updated and available for ease of use. Unlike instructors, your partners will need an additional layer of insight on the competitive landscape of the industry and the key differentiators between your product and others in the market. They will need education around your brand, messaging, pricing, and issues such as compliance. It's incredibly important that your partners are accurate. Remember, their customers are your customers.

Assess and Track

Consider using an LMS to deliver partner training and to track engagement with education. An LMS can help you to deliver an exceptional learning experience that is both effective for the customer and helps you meet your goals. While this is important with customers, it's arguably even more important when it comes to partners. They are representing you, so you need to make sure that they have accurate understanding and are achieving the desired results. Another great idea is to use some kind of video assessment tool, like Bongo, to check that partners are aligned with brand messaging. You can assess your partners through a simple video interface where they are given prompt-and-follow instructions to simulate a customer interaction. This can be used as an additional layer of quality control.

Whatever process you use, remember that you're deputizing these partners to go out into the world on your behalf. Whatever experience your customers have with your partners, that's how they will view your brand.

To get some wider thoughts on educating the team who will deliver the education, we reached out to Melissa VanPelt, vice president of Global Education and Advocacy at Seismic. She speaks below about must-ask questions for interviewing SMEs, as well as some best-practices for keeping your education team in line with the GTM strategy of the company.

Thoughts from . . . Melissa VanPelt, Vice President, Global Education and Advocacy at Seismic

When I think about choosing instructors at Seismic, I'll start by thinking about the content and its level of technicality. If the content is extremely technical, I might look to use SMEs, and make sure that we train them first with a workshop on training facilitation skills. However, much of our content targets functional platform knowledge that any person with a strong learning background should be able to grasp pretty quickly. So generally speaking, I put more emphasis on training expertise and skillset. While product expertise does drive credibility, training delivery can make or break the learner experience. Poor learner experience will equate to a frustrated learner and negative outcomes, as it takes your learners' neutral experience and adds frustration or negative emotions around the product itself. Experienced trainers will ensure that they are experts on the core content within the curriculum or topics they are covering. They'll also have a knack for building and delivering content in an easily consumable and digestible way that scaffolds complexity and breaks it down for the learner effectively. Often, it can be easier to train an educator on a specific product than it is to teach an SME how to deliver effective training. Ultimately, I feel that training ability is more important. It is a real craft, and I think I put more emphasis on having these skills in their toolbelt than having an SME who can answer any question under the sun. If possible, though, at Seismic we try to marry the two. We'll have a skilled facilitator deliver the training, and an SME on hand to answer any questions.

Nurturing the SME Relationship

The SME relationship is really critical. Our SMEs are our product managers or implementation delivery team, and they are super busy. They have their own full-time jobs, and supporting education isn't their top priority. We try to be very sensitive to this, and ensure that

(continued)

we always come prepared to a meeting, gathering as much information as possible ahead of time. Coming to the meeting knowledgeable about the topic, having read the technical documentation or GTM information that's available helps you to gain credibility and show that you've made an effort and you're cognizant that the SMEs time is valuable.

Some tips! Make sure to record them so that you can engage in a fluent dialogue and actively listen and ask questions, and so you can go back to the recording after the fact. It's also really important to be transparent about expectations and timelines, and to help them to understand how the work that you're doing is going to support the product launch and further adoption of the product. Set proper alignment on the shared performance outcomes you are jointly targeting and how the course will support those goals.

Education as Part of the Wider Organization at Large

At Seismic, we have a centralized Release Readiness program that is a strategic function and is dedicated to keeping key stakeholder groups informed on relevant information surrounding product release and roadmap. It is a tiger team made up of stakeholders from different orgs across our business; Product Management, Product Marketing, Sales Engineering, Enablement, Education, Implementation, Documentation, and so on. This team shares key information and tightly tracks and manages key dependencies, timelines, and deliverables so that each group can execute its activities surrounding product release in a coordinated way.

Customer education is a cross-functional effort across multiple touchpoints that will impact a customer's experience, their competency, and ultimately confidence working with your business or using your product. It is something that every customer-facing employee plays some role in, whether they know it or not. They are facilitating learning for our customers along the customer journey, whether that's pre- or post-sale. If we can think about customer education more globally, rather than just product training or Seismic University, or instructor-led training, every touchpoint with a prospective or existing customer is an opportunity to educate. It is therefore really important to create a seamless end-to-end learning experience. If you think about it, all functions have the same goals, increasing customer knowledge, confidence, and success with the product to ultimately drive retention and renewal. So I say start with the end goal (which is making the customer successful) and work backward, by fully recognizing and understanding the learning needs of our customers, and then addressing those needs through unified programs and people resources that enable our customers' success. This starts with educating your internal, customer-facing staff so that you hand over the same messaging to customers and partners.

They don't all need to know everything – for example, your GTM sales teams might need just the high-level, value-based messaging, while your implementation delivery team needs to go into more depth on feature functionality – but you want everyone to speak about the product in the same way so that the customer experience is fluent.

Educating Disparate Learner Audiences

Broadly speaking, we facilitate learning for our customers in two main ways: through educational products (like courses on Seismic University) and also through people resources (like our implementation staff). As a result, our customer education team is specifically responsible for building learning programs for three main audiences, the customer, our internal implementation delivery staff, and our external partner delivery staff. We target three main competency domains: tactical implementation, consulting competency, and product knowledge. The goal is to create reusable content that scales across all our different learner audiences. Some of the content is relevant to all three learner audiences, and other content is specific to a certain learner group. For example, all three will need

(*continued*)

product education, but our internal implementation delivery team will also need to learn about implementation methodology and internal processes, as well as the approach we use for onboarding and getting a customer live. Of course, a lot of this will be applicable to partners as well, but some of the process elements will differ. Another good example is the way that we target our implementation delivery teams with content that builds their consulting competency, so they have a strategic advisor skillset to best guide and support customers. We don't need to teach our partners how to be consultants. That is already their expertise. But we do need to teach them how to consult our customers on best practice Seismic implementation.

We may also validate their proficiency differently. The learning structure will likely be the same whether it is internal or external delivery staff – both will need to learn, practice, reflect, and certify – but the timelines and way in which they go about the activities in each of those workflows may differ. To manage the different needs, we've spent a lot of time moving toward more modular content. When we first started out, we weren't great at modularization, but as we've expanded the audiences we're targeting and our content portfolio, we've realized how important this is as a goal, and we've made a massive effort to modularize everything. This allows us to create "pick and packs" where we can reuse content for different personas and audiences, and also more easily translate and localize education as part of our global customer education strategy. Education at scale is the goal.

The success of your education will hinge on so many different relationships! Make sure that you have chosen competent instructors, forged relationships with SMEs, and aligned with the rest of the organization on the GTM strategy of the business. In the next chapter, we will turn our thoughts to practical considerations around UX and engagement when creating the learning experience itself.

10

Step 8: Design Learning Experiences That Lead to Behavioral Change

If you've ever taken an online course but felt frustrated by the clunky design of the learning platform, or attended a virtual training session but been distracted by the technology rather than the content, you'll know a few things about what stands in the way of optimal user experience. User experience (UX) in the context of learning is everything that occurs during learning, including the learner's subjective reaction to the experience as they interact with your learning materials and products. While good UX delights learners and generates a positive psychological state, bad UX will cause frustration and bring up negative emotions for the learner. These types of negative emotions have been shown to have a detrimental impact on motivation and learning.[1]

As a result, it's important to be mindful about the experience that you're crafting. If you create great content with a bad UX, the fact that the catalog is disorganized, that learners are distracted by extraneous content, or that they don't know where to click will be enough to negate the quality of the content and inhibit a customer's ability to learn.

UX also plays an important role when it comes to stickiness. Research from web design shows that you have 50 milliseconds to make an impression on your users.[2] That's no time at all. Your design needs to be clear and simple and engage learners extremely fast, or your learners will bounce.

To optimize for learning, look to eliminate all UX issues that aren't related to the learning itself, such as challenges with navigating the website or a lengthy sign-up process to get started. Ensure that the content is written in a way that will help learners to understand, eliminating industry jargon. Focus on delight and people will recommend your learning to others. For this to happen, you need to go beyond the content itself and think about how to ensure that learners enjoy the process of learning.

Utilizing Mayer's Principles

We've established that a good UX is key to increasing consumption and retention. However, just as UX designers won't conventionally have a background in instructional design or understanding how people learn, instructional designers may not have a deep grasp on UX design.

One way to bridge that gap is to look at the research of Richard E. Mayer, an educational psychologist whose research has formed the foundation of our understanding of multimedia instruction today.[3] Mayer laid out 12 principles (see Figure 10.1) that specifically address user experience

---

[1] Chai M. Tyng, Hafeez U. Amin, Mohamad N. M. Saad, and Aamir S. Malik, "The Influences of Emotion on Learning and Memory," *Frontiers in Psychology* 8 (2017): 1454, DOI=10.3389/fpsyg.2017.01454.

[2] Gitte Lindgaard, Gary Fernandes, Cathy Dudek, and J. Brown, "Attention Web Designers: You Have 50 milliseconds to Make a Good First Impression," *Behaviour & Information Technology* 25, no. 2 (2006): 115–126, DOI: 10.1080/01449290500330448.

[3] Richard E. Mayer, *Multimedia Learning*, 2nd 3d. (Cambridge: Cambridge University Press, 2009).

Figure 10.1 Mayer's 12 Principles of Multimedia Learning

design in the context of learning and the important role that UX plays in learning. We've separated these principles into three lessons that help to create learning experiences with UX front of mind.

Lesson 1: Avoid Extraneous Information

In this cluster of principles, Mayer discusses the need to stay focused on what the learner needs to know. Keep your visuals simple and relevant to the learning topic, and beware of fluff. Even if you think it's cute or funny – it might well be standing in the way of the learning experience. Ask yourself, "Am I still focused on my learning objective, or have I been pulled into a tangent?"

If you're using audio narration during your learning materials, like in a video, limit the amount of text you have on screen. While a person can visually look at graphics and still have room to listen, it's much harder to listen to narration and also read text. In some cases, you're less likely to understand the message if you're focusing on reading and listening, even if the text on the screen and the narration are the same words. If you do include text, this should be to highlight or signal the main takeaways, knowing that the learner's eyes will immediately be drawn to those words.

Mayer comments that humans learn best when there are only graphics and narration included, and that a best practice is to remove all text, but this is a situation where the best practice may come up against accessibility for your users. For a win/win scenario, look to create video content that uses narrated audio by default, but offers the option for people to turn on captioning.

Lesson 2: Minimize Cognitive Load

After eliminating anything that isn't relevant from your learning, Mayer turns to discussing how to present your content in a way that will minimize cognitive load, which refers to the total amount of information your working memory can hold at the same time. Too much cognitive load will make it far more difficult for learners to retain what they learn.

One of Mayer's principles, spatial contiguity, involves placing words and pictures that correspond to one another near each other, which makes it easier for learners to decipher meaning. For example, if you have a graph with sectors marked in specific colors, put the key directly underneath each color, not on the other side of the screen.

Next, corresponding words and visuals should be presented simultaneously rather than successively. This means if you're presenting an animation or a tutorial of how a feature works, layer the narration over the visuals at the same time. This will allow the learner to hold both in working memory and make a mental connection between the verbal and the visual. This approach has been proven to lead to better recall than following the instructions with the demonstration separately.

Mayer continues that people learn better when a message is split into segments, which we've discussed before with our concepts of chunking and microlearning. Here, Mayer adds that it's important to give the learner control over their consumption of the chunks of information and the pace of their learning, allowing them to go back and relearn something or pause at a point that makes sense to them. We've all experienced that moment where you're comprehending something that's been said, or thinking of an example it reminds you of, and suddenly you realize 15 seconds have gone by and you've missed what came next! Segmenting and providing control to the user reduces the likelihood of this happening, something that's far easier when creating eLearning than it is in ILT or VILT. The drive toward using videos for customer education makes it harder to segment content, and when the learners have to pause, move back and search for what they were looking for, the friction can become a real hindrance. When creating video content, ask instructors to try to incorporate this principle by pausing between topics, checking for understanding, or taking a moment to summarize and ask for questions.

You can also help to minimize cognitive load by offering some pre-training. Knowing the basics gives learners something to draw from and recall. Think about simple definitions or concepts that you can offer in an introductory video or a cheat sheet that can be emailed out before a course. This gives learners something to digest ahead of time that can prime them for deeper learning on the topic.

Lesson 3: Turn Up the Engagement Factor

Our final category involves encouraging your learners to pay attention and draw on their motivation to learn. Here, Mayer's principles recognize that humans learn best when there are visuals to back up text, as long as they are highly targeted to the learning objective. When thinking about tone, an informal, conversational voice is best, as learners are more likely to be drawn into the learning when they feel that they are playing an active part in the conversation. Look for opportunities for personalization, and keep it simple and casual.

When creating a narration, it's important to use audio that has been recorded professionally by a human, rather than rely on a computer-generated voice. It can be tempting to turn to software that can parse and read your content when considering cost and flexibility, but a computer voice has been proven to negatively impact learning. Perhaps one day we will have AI that is indistinguishable from the human voice, but we're not there yet! Use a good microphone, ensure your recording is good quality, and keep the human touch.

Last, let's talk talking heads, which are video segments of a person talking to the viewer. Who doesn't love using talking heads? They are a great way to make learning more personal and human and can be useful to set up introductions when there isn't an easy way to get started. However, it's important to recognize that humans will naturally look at other humans. That means if you use a picture-in-picture format where the video of the talking head is in the corner, your learners will be drawn to look at the face instead of the main screen. It's therefore best to use talking heads to provide a break between different slides or learning objectives and switch the talking head for narration alone where there is other content to focus on. Otherwise, you may find that you're competing for the learner's attention.

Learning Styles versus Learning Strategies

You may have heard the idea that when you're creating educational content, you need to consider all kinds of learning styles, whether that's for visual learners, auditory learners, or kinesthetic learners. However, this as nothing more than a pervasive myth, and the science backs it up![4] Studies show that there is no such thing as learning styles. There are certainly learning preferences, but there is no evidence that adapting your pedagogical approach to learning preferences will make any difference on learning transference or outcomes.

So, what does make a difference? Learning strategies. You'd be hard pressed to implement any learning strategy that is grounded in learning science and find it doesn't have some impact on increasing achievement and transference. Let's explore a few proven learning strategies in more detail.

Chunking, Assessment, and Feedback

Spacing learning out into smaller sections is a proven way to improve learning outcomes, as seen in Mayer's principle of segmenting learning above. *Cognitivism* explains that the brain can only hold so much information in working memory, so if you want people to learn, it's important to chunk information into similar themes or concepts.

At the end of each learning objective, formative assessments have been shown to reinforce learning and evaluate comprehension. Unlike summative assessments that take place at the end of training to gauge proficiency, formative assessments allow you to spot if there are gaps in knowledge that you can address through feedback or by giving more depth or insight into a topic at the moment.

Observational Learning

Especially when you're creating educational content for physical products or software, observational learning can be incredibly effective. Having someone show you how to use the product and complete a task with it can have a powerful impact on retention. This comes from Social Learning Theory and Albert Bandura's assertion that human behavior is learned

---

[4] Joshua Cuevas, "Is Learning Styles-Based Instruction Effective? A Comprehensive Analysis of Recent Research on Learning Styles," *Theory of Research in Education* 13, no. 3 (November 2015): 308–333.

through observation, imitation, and modeling, all of which have a primal role in the way we retain information.[5]

Gamification

Gamification is a fantastic learning strategy in which designers apply game-like elements to non–game contexts using game design thinking. Examples are points, badges, leaderboards, and winning streaks, to name just a few. This strategy works because of operant conditioning, where rewards and punishments have been proven to moderate behavior. Humans experience endorphins when they earn a reward, and aversion when they do something wrong. You can look at the works of B. F. Skinner to learn more about this theory.

Storytelling

Human brains are wired for storytelling. We store memories based on patterns and relationships between ideas, and this impacts how we experience the world. Storytelling involves implementing a four-step structure of narrative, which starts with a beginning, continues to a problem, offers a resolution, and then suggests an ending. This all forms a mental map and makes learning easier. This is the case whether we're talking about math, science, history, or your product. This strategy is well-grounded in neuroscience. When you watch a video with bullets of information, that's stimulating the language processing part of your brain. When you hear a story, your brain becomes lit up with emotional regulation. The best stories, those that really engage and rivet us, produce neurochemicals in our brains that have been shown to strengthen focus, motivation, and memory. Include stories where possible, especially during the "why" of a presentation. Just remember that stories are also distinctly cultural. The stories that work for an American audience don't always work for other audiences!

---

[5] Albert Bandura, *Social Learning Theory* (Englewood Cliffs, NJ: Prentice Hall, 1977).

Discussion Boards and Chatrooms

If you can, provide an opportunity for learners to discuss content with one another, either in real time – such as using breakout rooms for VILT or small discussion groups in person – or within a community forum, such as after an online course. This strategy is backed up by some modern theories around communities of practice, first proposed by cognitive anthropologist Jean Lave and educational theorist Etienne Wenger in their book *Situated Learning*.[6] The book posits that learning is fundamentally a social process, and when you're part of a community who are doing the same kinds of learning that you are, this can boost retention, motivation, and transference.

The closer your learning experience is to its real-world context, the more you will have access to other professionals who are a community of practice for your learners and the more opportunities you will have to strengthen and consolidate learning. A community of like-minded people is a powerful way of exponentially improving learning on a topic, providing a social fabric for learning, suggesting expanded points of discussion, and offering knowledgeable peers and advanced learners who can act as teachers.

Practical Considerations for Creating Education Content

One decision you'll need to make at this point is to decide what tools you're going to use to create the content. This usually falls between two options – native authoring tools that are inside your LMS, or SCORM, which stands for Sharable Content Object Reference Model.

With native authoring tools, you usually get a WYSIWYG (What You See Is What You Get) editor that allows you to picture exactly what your content will look like in production, and you can very easily format text, insert media content, and utilize add-ons such as widgets or roles, all of which are native to the system. As you're using standard content formats, your time to market is likely to be a lot quicker, and you'll be able to adapt or reuse this content for other channels or use cases, such as emailing out a

---

[6] Jean Lave and Etienne Wenger, *Situated Learning: Legitimate Peripheral Participation (Learning in Doing: Social, Cognitive and Computational Perspectives)* 1st ed. (Cambridge: Cambridge University Press, 1991).

PDF or adding a video to your website. You can also change small elements as and when you need, as this content has been created in a modular way.

On the other side of the equation, you have SCORM. As it hasn't been created natively, this format allows you to create online training content that can be shared across systems. SCORM is used to create design-heavy, interactive, and immersive training modules using authoring tools like Adobe Captivate and Articulate Storyline, design tools that allow you to use animations and get a lot more interactive with what you create. When you've finished building the content, it gets packaged into a SCORM file, which, in most cases, allows you to place it directly into your LMS.

Working Out Which Content Authoring Tools to Use

Like many decisions, the choice of content authoring tools comes down to what your goals are. SCORM isn't lightweight, so this kind of content will take a long time to develop, and in the moment – it can take a while to load, too! SCORM isn't super device-friendly either, so if you're looking to create an omnichannel learning experience you will likely want to stick to native authoring tools. You're also going to lose your eye in the sky when it comes to reporting and analytics. As your SCORM content is created outside of your LMS, it can become a blind spot. You won't know where users gave up or became frustrated and you won't be able to track information like quiz scores as easily. For a short, engaging experience that's design-heavy, however, SCORM is a perfect fit.

In our experience the best approach for customer education is one in which you're mixing and matching to suit your needs, blending both SCORM and native authoring tools. You can create a lightweight, easy-to-build lesson with text, images and video, flip cards, and quizzes – and then when you click Next, you load up a SCORM file that is integrated into the experience, something like a game to practice what you've just learned which you couldn't have created natively. Once your users have completed the mini experience, they click Next again, and return to the natively authored experience.

As the industry continues to grow in maturity, we'll likely see some changes. Many LMS providers are already acquiring or creating robust authoring tools that create SCORM content as native authoring features within their platform. Additionally, as LMS tools invest more in content authoring tools, which are modern, sleek, and easy to use, customers will be able to get as close as you could imagine to a truly delightful interactive learning experience without the use of SCORM. As a result, while the current ecosystem is that there are native authoring tools that allow you to attach SCORM into the LMS, in 10 years we'll likely be seeing a convergence of these two platforms where all content is authored directly from your LMS – deeply integrated, equally lightweight, and with analytics included.

Linear versus Nonlinear Navigation

The way in which your learners navigate the learning experience is another important decision. It can feel intuitive to create a linear experience, where you can only move to the next step once you've completed the previous one. In that way, you can ensure that they've grasped one concept before they move onto the next. However, unless there is prerequisite knowledge that the learner needs before they can move through the learning path, this could be a mistake. Many learners, especially younger generations of learners, are drawn to being able to skip around and engage with content in the way that is convenient and comfortable to them. They feel confined by being closely locked into a sequential path. By locking one course until you complete another, you may see steep completion drop-offs.

The practical solution is therefore to unlock your content and allow for nonlinear navigation of your learning to accommodate both learning preferences. Make sure to organize your content to offer a recommended sequential path with a clear hierarchy between the courses to explain the ideal way in which they are meant to be consumed. However, allow people to skip around, so that if they are uninterested in a certain lesson or come to your course with a certain amount of knowledge already, they can skip what feels redundant or less engaging.

One customer education team that's doing great things with UX design is Snyk. Manager of Customer Education Michele Wiedemer gave us some insight on how she creates the content and the experience of her education projects.

Thoughts from . . . Michele Wiedemer, Manager of Customer Education at Snyk.io

In a fast-paced company, we remind our product team that if a feature isn't documented, it doesn't exist. When I joined Snyk, I wanted to extend that to say, "If users don't know how to use a feature – it doesn't exist." In a similar way, education itself may as well not exist if users can't find it. It's even worse if learners have difficulty with a learning experience, such as finding it difficult to navigate. That scenario may negatively affect their sentiment toward the product itself. So, it's vital that we consider the user experience for learning. The idea of empathy for what the learners need is really core for me, and it always informs my work as I start a new project.

Minimizing Cognitive Load and Maximizing Engagement

My core practices originate from the Information Mapping™ methodology, which I learned early in my career. In addition to thinking about the user's needs, I try to separate the content or learning activity by its purpose.

Sometimes I need to deliver a ton of information. But too much at once can be overwhelming, and the learner simply won't retain it. For example, we've all seen slides with way too much on them (one of my personal pet peeves). I like to think of a slide – whether in an instructor-led course or in online self-paced learning – as a visual hook. Instead of asking the learner to read more than a few words, I let the words of the instructor or narrator guide the learning. I include one or two simple images to give learners something to remember. If words need to be there, such as with a labeled diagram, I lean on Mayer's principle of proximity to help the learner see how the words and the pictures are associated.

Of course, there is a place for online learning activities that are reading-based. However, I try to find ways to break up large chunks of information. Even if my options are limited, formatting choices like subheadings, paragraph breaks, step numbers, and a few images can make a difference. If I have the opportunity, some version of a click-to-reveal activity can work well with text, too.

Another related Mayer's principle is the coherence principle. Sometimes there is a tendency to want to give students every piece of information they could possibly need on a given topic. But this tendency can easily turn into those 30- or 60-minute information dump sessions that can't in good conscience be called training. So I try to think about what the learners need at this point. What will help them have early success with a handful of tasks?

I am often guided by the fact that learners don't usually *have* to be here. This isn't compliance training, or forced attendance. So, while we rely on some amount of intrinsic motivation to get customers to learn, we still have to sell it to them a little bit. I do this by always thinking about the WIIFM – What's In It For Me? Even in a short, two-minute video, I help the learner know what to expect from this learning experience. I try to find a short sentence that immediately pulls them in with a "Yes. I want to be here. This interests me."

It's also much harder to keep the customer engaged if there are too many topics without any chance for breaks or reflection. Besides the engagement factor, there are benefits to separating topics. It's easier for the content creator and reviewers to create and maintain that content, and it's easier for the learner to process, by providing a chance to consolidate that learning before moving on. It also makes it easy for learners to come back for a refresher if they need it.

A recent experience illustrates why it's not a good idea to include too many topics at once. I signed up for a new product, and got the welcome email with a two-minute "Getting Started" video. I wasn't exactly sure how I would be using the product, but I knew that it would help me solve a particular kind of problem. So, I was eager to learn. Unfortunately, I couldn't tell you one thing the video included. Some best practices were there. The WIIFM was there at the beginning of the video. The length was short. But it included a

(*continued*)

tour of everything the tool could do. The title of the video could have been "The Massive Tour of Absolutely Everything." As a result, by trying to include all the information, it succeeded in informing me of nothing.

Audio presentation also matters. The video that arrived in my inbox included rather monotone narration. No matter how engaging the visuals are, the instructor or narrator can drive a learner away in seconds. When I'm recording narration, I try to make it sound like I'm having a conversation with the viewer. Even though I'm reading from a script, the tone and cadence of my speaking voice provides cues for the learner, saying, "Hey, listen up! I'm telling you something important!" in a really approachable way.

Often, You'll Need to Use What You Have

Sometimes, even though I know that learning strategies, products, or tools will be effective, I have to work with what I've got. Gamification, observational learning, SCORM tools, lab environments . . . they all have their place. However, I haven't let the time and resources available or the budget of the project discourage me. I find that for most scenarios, there are multiple ways to reach the learners.

Of course, over the years I've built preferences for certain tools and products. I rely on Camtasia and Snagit on a regular basis, and I've found that you can do a lot with those. When I have a platform available for hosting SCORM, I've also used some of the rapid eLearning authoring tools (like Captive, Storyline, and Rise). But when I don't have the ideal tool available, I try to find a new route to accomplish the objectives. I love that about the customer education world – we're big, creative problem solvers. When we hit a "No," we don't let that stop us. We just move on to find the "Yes!"

We hope this chapter has provided a good overview on how to create content with best-practice UX in mind, and provided some learning strategies that you can lean on to create your own programs. Now it's time to get your education into the hands of your learners by creating a smart distribution strategy.

11

Step 9: Make Sure Your Customers Consume Your Content

A clear distribution plan is a must-have when creating educational content, and yet a lot of people skip this step and go straight to measuring the impact of the education. So much effort and resources are put into creating content, and not nearly enough are given to distributing and marketing and making sure the content gets consumed. That's one of the reasons why we made this a discrete step in the *playbook*: not only having a content consumption and distribution strategy, but also understanding the channels that are available to you.

Go Back to Your Learning Personas

Take a step back and remember all of that work you have done around learning personas. Who have you created this content for? What do they need to know? If you haven't already considered where they are going to engage with your content, and when they need to know this information – now is the time. You might need to take your content and chop it up into smaller parts so that they aren't receiving more information than they need at this juncture. You'll want to make sure that your distribution strategy is aligned with their needs. For example, if they're an admin user, maybe the best way to reach them is in product. However, if they're an executive buyer – email might be a smarter choice. It's all about marketing your content in channels that will reach the customer.

Answering: WIIFM?

"What's in it for me?" This is a question that you want your learners to have the answer to within seconds. What will they get out of your content, and why should they care? This is where you want to grab your marketing hat and make the landing page or marketing content intrinsically compelling. When done right, this taps into the learner's desire to achieve success with the platform and thereby their own role. Here are a few examples of tactics you can use to drive consumption:

Keep It Simple   On course detail pages, minimize information and concisely tell the story of why this course is of value to the learner. For articles, you might have a top line that explains "In this article you will learn," and then follows it up with bullet points. You need to allow people who are constantly making decisions about where to invest their time to make a quick judgment call that this is worthwhile content.

Talking Heads   Short videos of someone talking can be used on course details pages to great effect. Use someone who is potentially a familiar face, perhaps the same person you use elsewhere in the curriculum, and make it personable and human. This should be short – ideally under a minute – and explain a little about why the learner should care about what they are going to learn.

Sneak Peeks   In some cases, especially if you're monetizing content, it might not be enough to say, "In this course you will learn …" A minute-long video might not be enough to encourage the learner to make a purchase. In these situations, a sneak peek can be a great way to capture attention and give learners a taste of what they'll learn, plus allow them to kick the tires of the experience. Be careful about what you offer free of charge – you don't want to give away the good stuff for free!

Actively Promoting Your Content

You've clarified who your audience is, what's in it for them, and created a value proposition. Now you need to reach these customers by forming a plan for active promotion. Here's where a good relationship or an alliance with the marketing and product teams can be useful.

Forging Alliances Across the Organization

If you have the buy-in of the marketing teams, then you have support from all the distribution channels that they own, such as email, website, or social media. At Asana we found one of the most successful ways to reach customers was through a 30-day email nurture campaign. Emails were sent out on a schedule, Day 1, 2, 5, 9, and so on, and each email introduced a new concept, layering more complexity over time on how to get the most value out of using the product.

With product teams, you can figure out if they have ways to promote content within the product itself. In-context learning can be a powerful way to promote and distribute educational content, reaching out to the customer in their moment of need. However, product teams may be protective of the experience, or might not have access to digital adoption tools that provide ways to send messages using event triggers. At the very least, you can ensure that your education is promoted through a robust help menu in-product, or within the product release notes or product newsletter. Consider whether this is a good fit for promoting your content or if you want to create your own learning newsletter on the academy or on the learning site explicitly designed to deliver learning and promote new education.

You also want to create a strong relationship with customer support and customer success. These stakeholders are optimally placed to channel your content to customers when they need it, whether that's to resolve a ticket, support onboarding, or provide deeper meaning or context. You might find they are one of your best resources.

Lastly, think about professional services. At Optimizely, we found that trainers who sat on the education team had invested so much time creating a training experience that helped customers get to value quickly that we could package it into an offering in professional services. Rather than attend open, ad-hoc webinars and download or share disparate content in an unstructured way, we could offer customers the chance to purchase a complete, customized, or tailored education package.

Optimizing Your Content for Consumption

How is your content organized and categorized on the website itself? Think about your catalog and how easy it is for learners to navigate. You want to create a highly organized, visual hierarchy that is easy to scan and browse. When they finish one course, what's next? Make sure that you include a strong call to action (CTA) from one piece of content to the next, whether that's directly at the end of a video or article or included in the email that contains their certificate of completion. The main thing is to never leave the learner guessing. Without offering a clear learning path, you're simply adding cognitive load and increasing the likelihood that your customers will feel overwhelmed and confused. When learners are left to figure out what's next for themselves, they're much more likely to drop out.

If you're using a platform like Thought Industries, you'll have the ability to create and provide learner notifications without needing to draw on marketing resources or product teams. You'll be able to set up automation that sends notifications to learners when they complete a course and encourages them to take the next step. This can have a really powerful impact on learners continuing their education.

Of course, different learners will often have different needs, and in that case there might not be an exact next step to point them toward. In this situation, you might want to offer an inflection point, depending on their needs, that will provide a selection of courses and allow them to choose which one they want to learn next.

Information Architecture

Organizing content in a way that's easily scannable and browsable is a design skill, and there's a lot of information out there to help you ground your navigation in best practices. The science of organizing and structuring content is known as information architecture (IA). The goal of IA in customer education should be that learners can quickly and easily adjust to your content and find everything that they need without friction. There are three organizational structures to choose from:

1. *Hierarchical.* Presenting content in a way that makes it immediately obvious what should be the most important to the learner. Do this with headers or visuals or the order of the information.
2. *Sequential.* Great for learning paths with prerequisites, or where one action should follow another. You'll create the content in such a way that a learner can move from one section to the next with ease.
3. *Matrix.* Allowing users to choose for themselves how they want to organize content in a way that makes sense to them. Offer filters so learners can manage their own content, whether that's alphabetically, by content, by audience, or with another choice entirely.

Searching for Content

If you acknowledge that your content lives in different places, whether that's your website, your knowledge base, or even in unstructured places like on a community thread, then you need to accept that there is a pain point for learners in searching across systems to find answers to what they need to know. There's a growing awareness of this challenge, and many organizations are looking for a way to meet it head-on with a unified or federated search system.

There are two main options at the moment. The first is to manually go into search fields in all the various locations and index with relevant keywords before attaching them to the relevant resources. The second is to go with a vendor such as Search Unify, which has the technology to crawl through all of your data and combine this into a single search result page. Over time, it is likely that we will see more systems and partnerships being put in place. For example, a community platform might form a partnership with an LMS platform and allow both of their search engines to crawl one another's data.

No matter what, it's important to recognize that your learners are often going to fall back on searching via Google, as it's just the most user-friendly, intuitive, and habit-forming method of search. As a result, you can't get away without a sound SEO strategy for your education. Optimizing your educational content for search on the web means thinking about keywords that match the user's intent. When you're creating the titles and descriptions for course content, certification landing pages, webinar recordings, and virtual conferences – consider keywords and optimize on-page elements such as the title, heading tags, meta description, file names, and image descriptions where relevant, and include links to other sites and pages, especially those that have a high domain authority. Don't forget that search engines won't be able to crawl any hidden or protected content such as anything in a PDF or behind a paywall. It can therefore be helpful to create a summary of your content as a landing page or overview to encourage traffic in the right direction. At the end of this chapter, Alessandra Marinetti discusses the balance of searchability versus ability to track and measure content in an LMS or behind a paywall.

What's Your Content Channel Strategy?

You might find yourself asking, "Where is this content going to go?" It can be helpful to have a clear content channel strategy that gives you insight into the overarching goals of each channel and what you're striving to accomplish. Of course, you may end up distributing content in multiple channels, but it's useful to have a framework. If you have an asset that's about building awareness or generating some hype around a new feature, your support channels won't be the best fit – it's more likely to fit on social media.

Typically, there are three kinds of channels: marketing, training, and support. Marketing will help you to attract new customers and convert them into paying customers from trial or free subscriptions. Your marketing channels, like your blog, email marketing, or social media, will deepen the engagement for existing customers. If you develop content for this goal – focused on the value proposition and not at all technical – marketing is probably the way to go. In contrast, if you're looking to distribute more technical content, such as get-started guides and tutorials – anything designed to reduce friction on using the product – your support channels will be a good place to start. This is your knowledge base or help center, the places your customers go to troubleshoot their challenges. As already mentioned, you might also choose to distribute support content in the product so it can surface in context.

The final category is training content. This channel is your academy. Here's where customers develop product mastery and unlock the true potential of your product's value. If your content is attempting to drive behavioral change, your training channels are where to push it through.

A Word on Email Marketing   Customer education is well-placed to contribute to marketing channels such as the company blog, social media, and even email marketing. However, if you're thinking about distributing your content through email, it's important to acknowledge that your customers are being bombarded with a lot of communications via this channel. One idea is to use trigger-based email campaigns, which can ensure that the messages are more relevant to the customer and that they arrive at the right time. For example, if the customer engages with the reporting function in the product, send an email that features a video on how to use reporting. You can A/B test exactly how to make this happen (for example, whether to send the email to anyone who uses reports or only to those who churn halfway through the process). While some companies simply automate email campaigns at set intervals, it can be difficult to predict when customers will reach certain stages, and it can quickly get overwhelming for the customer if you're feeding them the wrong information or education.

Your Pricing Strategy Is Part of Your Distribution Strategy

We mentioned back in Chapter 2 that approximately 75 percent of training content is fee-based, while 25 percent is free. Think back to your business model now. If the content that you're distributing is in the fee-based bucket, you'll need to decide how you're going to price it.

A lot goes into figuring out the right price. The first thing you need to think about is how much the content cost you to make. Obviously, this is your baseline. You don't want to be losing money on your education. If you choose to charge cost-based pricing, you'll usually add a margin of 10 to 20 percent. A lot of companies stop here. They may have a directive or a goal to meet a certain profit level, and adding that margin will meet that goal, so they don't go any further. However, it's important to develop your muscles around market-based pricing and value-based pricing. Do an analysis and see what the demand in the market is like, and you may be able to justify a higher price tag. Also think about the value that you're providing. Customer education expert and GM at ServiceRocket Bill Cushard often speaks about looking for the outcome you're providing to the customer when you price your content. If someone can take your course and get a $10,000 pay rise at their next role, wouldn't that be worth $500? If an executive can get more value out of a $100,000 software subscription, isn't that worth $5,000?

When you do arrive at your price point, start high. See if you're gaining traction with your pricing, and if not, you can add a discount or go lower. It's much harder to raise pricing if you see that the course has good traction. You could also start off with a limited-time discount, such as 20 percent off for the first month or the first six months. We'll talk more about how to tweak your monetization strategy in Chapter 13 when we discuss improving education.

How Will You Package Your Content?

Once you've chosen your pricing, you'll also need to decide how you're going to package the education. Here are four options to consider:

A la Carte   Price each course or content individually, and charge a set price for it up front. The fee may allow the learner full access, or it may provide access for a specific and limited amount of time.

Bundles   These are collections of individual courses that are sold as a single unit. They may cover a specific learning path or be aimed at a specific type of user. For example, you might offer a Developer bundle or an Admin bundle.

Training Credits   Training credits can be purchased ahead of time, then redeemed on any other content, a la carte or bundled. You might decide to offer a discount to encourage learners to buy up front training credits that they can then use on training of their choice.

Subscriptions   If you offer a subscription to training content, users will typically sign up for a monthly or annual package (with annual packages usually provided at a discount) where they have all access to set content, on-demand. You can set up subscriptions for specific courses, for your whole academy, or anywhere in between.

Considering Accessibility in Distribution

Over 61 million adults in the US alone have a disability. When you think of your customers, remember that a sizable portion will need your content to be accessible and inclusive.

Accessibility Ideas That Are Simple to Implement

People sometimes talk about how it's too hard to make changes to their content to include multiple needs, or say that they don't have the resources. The research of Dr. Sheryl Burgstahler is a great place to start if you're look-ing for easy ways to implement changes when you're creating and distribut-ing content, and we'll add a few tips and tricks here, too.[1]

Optimize for Screen Readers.   A screen reader scans the page the same way as a person does, so it's important to have consistent layouts, including clear headers and the same fonts throughout. Make sure to use the alt text function to provide a description of images, too.

Use Descriptive Wording for Hyperlinks.   A screen reader will also tab all hyperlinks for easy navigation. Let's say we have the sentence, "Learn more about how to build a website here." People often use the word "here" or the phrase "learn more" for their hyperlinks, but when all the links from the content are placed in one group, this means nothing to the consumer. Instead, use the descriptive part of the text for the hyperlink, such as "how to build a website."

---

[1] Sheryl Burgstahler, "Equal Access: Universal Design of Instruction," Disabilities, Opportunities, Internetworking, and Technology, University of Washington, 2020, https://www.washington.edu/doit/equal-access-universal-design-instruction.

Caption Your Videos!   This is such an easy way to make sure that those with hearing disabilities can consume your content – if you're not doing this, you should be.

Consider Color-Blindness.   According to Color Blind Awareness, color vision deficiency impacts 1 in 12 men and 1 in 200 women. Worldwide, this is more than 300 million people. Use color combinations with high contrast, and try to avoid lots of reds and greens, which is a common challenge for those who struggle with color deficiencies.

Provide Multiple Ways for People to Learn.   Use a combination of text, video, audio, and images. This is not just a great way to be accessible to your learners, it's also a sound practice from an instructional design perspective.

Localizing Education Content

If you train customers internationally, you'll also want to consider your localization strategy. While the content and the delivery strategy may change, remember that the goals of the content should remain the same – supporting customers in doing their jobs at greater quality, with more efficiency and more accuracy.

Localization will likely start with translating your content. As translation can be expensive and time-consuming, stick to the 80/20 rule and only translate what's absolutely necessary or even look for opportunities to condense multiple pieces of content into one. Concentrating on core content saves you time and makes it easier for you to get to market with your materials faster. Make sure that you use a native-speaking local partner to review your translations for accuracy and nuance.

Another idea is to take a step down, technologically speaking, moving from videos to text-based content, or from eLearning to ILT. This means you can test your translated content in different regions before spending too much time on finalizing your education.

Translation is just step one. Don't underestimate how important culture is in localizing your content strategy. For example, training may assume a top-down management style, but in some regions, this just won't suit the audience. Interactivity may work in one location and not in another. Another example is humor. Laughter can play a large role in the learning experience, but what's funny for your local learners may fall flat abroad, and vice versa. The main thing to remember is that your audience won't adapt to you, they'll just drop out – so you need to meet them where they are.

Next, think about the available technology in the region. Will your learners have easy access to fast internet to download heavy-duty graphics or to engage with video-streaming content? If the course is meant to be viewed on a computer or laptop, will it work as well in a region where people rely heavily on mobile devices, like many emerging economies do?

Don't forget to think about how you will measure your success in different countries. Consider whether you're going to use the same metrics, and how you will make space in your community for customers from different regions so that you can ensure you're getting useful and broad feedback. In some cases, you may be able to leverage your LMS to provide advanced solutions for localization, including translation, easy management and universal updating or distribution of content, and localization of the user interface or learning experience, all from within the platform itself.

Effectively and impactfully distributing content is a huge topic! Alessandra Marinetti is the senior director of AppDirect Academy, and she shares her thoughts about aligning distribution to organizational and customer goals, and how to work with departments across the business to create a strong distribution strategy.

Thoughts from . . . Alessandra Marinetti, Senior Director, AppDirect Academy

Whenever I think about how to distribute education content, I consider the strategy from two perspectives. First – what is my company looking to achieve by distributing this content? And second – the WIIFM (What's in it for me?) of the customer. What does the customer need, and what will they best respond to?

(continued)

This starts by understanding my company's organizational goals, and also my distinct customer personas. The organization might want to speed up the onboarding process and get customers using the product quickly. In that case, I might create a quick video-based approach and push that out via marketing automation channels. However, if my persona is a developer who is more likely to be interested in technical documentation, in that case I'll switch my content strategy to something more text-based, and in terms of distribution, I could serve that via the community or knowledge base. As you can probably see, the process of creating a distribution strategy goes hand-in-hand with building a strategy for the content and the curriculum as a whole.

Work with Additional Departments for Content Distribution

I like to start by identifying the mechanisms the company already has for customer communications, and then look for opportunities to leverage them using existing channels.

One example is working with the product team to provide contextual in-app tours using technology like Pendo or WalkMe. This is a very effective way to distribute text or video-based content right at the time of need and without ever leaving the product. I find in-app content to be a compelling distribution strategy, as it can allow you to segment the education you're offering based on what your users need. At Box, we worked closely with the marketing and business intelligence teams to implement in-app modals to both advertise new training content and match specific content with unique personas based on how they were using the application. This way, we were able to target our audience with more precision and train them based on what they were looking to achieve. We were also able to quickly identify campaigns that weren't working and change our targeting or content approach.

Other examples of working with different departments for effective distribution include leaning on the marketing team to send content through newsletters, including the content in automated onboarding and nurture campaigns, or partnering with CSMs to leverage their deep knowledge of the customer needs and objectives to recommend learning tracks that align with their business needs. For example, at AppDirect, we work with CSMs to incorporate training in their Success Plans, which recommend the progression of training, depending on who the customer persona might be, and at what stage they are at in terms of the customer journey and their business needs. Ideally, CSMs should also be taking the training so that they can speak to its value and content in a knowledgeable way.

While basic information can be distributed via email or automation channels, as your content becomes more sophisticated, you may also want to think about how you can use other teams to help describe and confirm its value. This is especially important when you're incorporating education as part of support bundles or professional services, ensuring that sales teams promote the existence and benefits of training when they speak to prospects. Great training can get lost if it isn't championed across the organization when stakeholders speak to prospects and customers.

Ensure Content Is Discoverable for Customers

If you're using an LMS to distribute education, it's important to consider the impact on SEO. Think about optimizing searchability for users by making some quick videos, knowledge base articles, or even blog content that you're not gating and perhaps you don't even need to track consumption for. Then, use this content to generate interest for the training and certifications that you're hosting in your LMS, which makes it easy to track and measure, despite being less discoverable initially.

(continued)

You also need to think about creating content where your customers already are. While landing pages can be great for SEO and attracting prospects, existing customers are less likely to go to your website to find content. At Box, we promoted and created awareness for education within our Community and Support platform, which is where customers go to file tickets and look for information, so that they could see our latest training and certifications where we knew that they would already be.

Remember, optimizing content consumption for customers is largely about reducing friction. Features like single sign-on (SSO) into the LMS through your application can make it easier to access your content. Sometimes, you will need to look at trade-offs between ease of access for your more tactical content (for example, through YouTube) and the ability to track through an LMS.

Advice on Creating a Global Distribution Strategy

There are no two ways about it – localization is a bear! If you're just dipping your toes into localizing content, you might want to start with easier content such as text-based education. Begin with knowledge base articles or content built with Articulate Rise, for example, which is easy to maintain and change. In a SaaS-based product, this is really important, as you're likely to be working with a rapid release cycle, and it's paramount that your content is up to date.

If scale is less of an issue, but you need to be able to localize training, think about live online classes, or VILT. With virtual training, there's no travel involved – and all you need is a competent trainer who speaks the language. When I was working at LinkedIn, we leveraged CSMs who worked in that region and spoke the language. They were already experts on the platform, and were a great choice when content didn't need to be offered on-demand and scale for the non-English speaking audience wasn't an issue.

Ultimately, ask yourself – how essential is it for us to localize this content? Are the majority of your end-users proficient enough in

English to engage with your original content? Maybe you can get away without localization for a while. If not, start with the easy, text-based content, and then progressively expand to high-value content such as onboarding, or wherever your biggest pain point falls. As always, balance this with organizational goals. If localization is a really important strategy for the business, and you see the potential for strong ROI, you may want to look into outsourcing to a localization agency.

Optimizing your content for consumption and creating a clear and intelligent distribution and monetization strategy is easy to miss, and yet it is essential before you can meaningfully take the next step – measuring the success of the education that you've created.

12

Step 10: Did It Work? Measuring the Success of Your Content

We talk to a lot of customer education leaders about their challenges, and time and time again we hear one significant pattern. Customer education practitioners are creating a lot of training content, but they find it monumentally difficult to understand, demonstrate, and communicate the impact of the work that they do. In fact, according to our research at Thought Industries, 43 percent of our audience are struggling to measure the impact of their learning and training initiatives, with no change from one year to the next.

Being able to measure the impact of your education falls into two categories. First, assess the success for the customer. How much of your education has been consumed? Did your customers learn from the education, did they enjoy it, and did they change their behavior as a result? And second, has your program paid off for the business – has it shown return on investment (ROI)? We'll talk about ROI and how to explain your value to the C-suite in Step 12 (Chapter 14). For now, let's think about measuring customer learning, so we can see if your education is hitting the mark.

Data Doesn't Have to Be Hard!

There is a mental model prevalent in the customer education world that data and measurement are really hard. We're going to refute that claim right here and now, because while there are levels of complexity with everything – data doesn't have to be hard. If you focus too much on the ideal, where all of your data is visualized, triangulated, and connected and you have a clear view of the impact of all of your education, it's easy to allow the scope of the project to put you off. Not only that, but if you focus on the data that you can't measure, you're going to miss a lot of what you're already measuring.

The trick is to start simple. Start by choosing something to measure, and then trust that as your program becomes more mature, you'll naturally be able to add sophistication and roll in additional metrics. The main thing is to start with something!

Creating a Data Dictionary Using Kirkpatrick's Model of Evaluation

A data dictionary is a centralized repository of information where you have all your metrics defined, easily shareable, and classified by meaning to your organization. You could use anything from a spreadsheet to a task management platform to build it, but the idea is to be able to easily derive meaning from your data and see the relationship between the metric and the goals you have for your platform. In this context, once you have a thorough data dictionary, you have collected all the operational metrics that will help you to understand the health of your program.

To get this information, you're going to need to put in a lot of manual work chasing down data, digging through spreadsheets and reporting tools, and speaking to other areas of the business. You're definitely going to need to prioritize what data you collect, or you can quickly feel overwhelmed.

One framework that is really useful is an adapted version of the Kirkpatrick Model of Evaluation, which always helps our team get some understanding around what data we need and how this aligns with the different kinds of questions we might be asking about our education program.

The Kirkpatrick Model of Evaluation was developed in the 1950s to help L&D teams with corporate training, and it is still highly relevant today. The original model consisted of four levels: Reaction, Learning, Behavior and Results.[1] To best translate this model into the customer education world, it has become common to augment these levels with additional steps. Others have adapted and added new measurement options to its design. While some envision the model as a pyramid, it can be helpful to think of it as a funnel, with each level going deeper, but not necessarily foundational to the one before. Let's look at the model in detail (Figure 12.1), including the addition of Engagement as level zero, and touch on ROI as level 5.

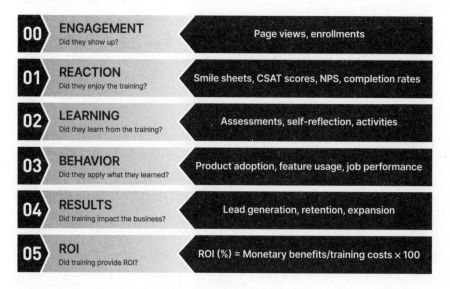

Figure 12.1 Adapted Kirkpatrick Model

---

[1] Donald Kirkpatrick, *Evaluating Training Programs: The Four Levels* (San Francisco: Berrett-Koehler, 1994).

Level Zero: Engagement

At this formative stage, your questions should be based on whether the customer is engaging with your content. You'll be looking at data such as page views and enrollments to articles or courses. We wrote in Chapter 11 about creating a strategy for distributing your content, and this is a really essential continuation of that step. While understanding the impact of education is paramount, before you even get there you need to make sure that learning gets into the customer's hands. If you can gauge that a high number of specific customers are consuming your content, and you accept that being educated helps your customers to achieve success, then it's clear that reach is a key metric to measure.

When done right, tracking and measuring your consumption can provide an unambiguous signal for how effectively your learners are finding your content and how deeply they are engaging once they find it. Other metrics around your content, such as CSAT or completion rates, can be high, but that isn't necessarily a sign that you're getting enough traction or ROI from your material. That's why, according to Maria Manning-Chapman, VP of Research Education Services at TSIA, even if you can't do anything else at all, "start by getting your arms around who is consuming and who isn't." Manning-Chapman calls this penetration rate data and provides a way to slice and dice this information into three pools, getting progressively more specific.

Breadth   First, look at what percentage of your customer accounts have at least one person who has consumed educational content. This is also known as account or install-base penetration rate. If at least one person from every account is educated, hopefully that person will share their knowledge with others. This person becomes your internal expert.

Depth   Next, what percentage of all customers in a single account has consumed educational content? This allows you to see whether you're going deep into each of your accounts, educating many users. This can be extremely helpful if your product is touching many different teams, to uncover, for example, that there is just a single user consuming content in a company – not enough to suggest meaningful interaction with your education. Here you need to think about how you can extend your reach, because if a single advocate or active learner in a company leaves, your position may suddenly become insecure.

Volume For individuals who are consuming content, how much do they consume on average? This can be answered by the number of content objects (e.g., number of courses completed), as well as with time spent consuming content. You'll also look at patterns with volume, such as when users are dropping out or how long they're spending on your content. If users are spending a long time on a course but aren't consuming much content, you might deduce that they are "stuck" somewhere, and it might help to break down that course into more digestible bites.

One number rarely tells a story. Once you have all three measurements, you can cross-reference the data to get a better picture of what's happening, such as looking at the percentage of accounts with at least one user who has completed an entire learning path – using breadth and also volume together for more powerful insights.

Chapman also suggests that you consider using categories of active, underactive, and inactive users to help more easily understand your reach metrics. For example, if you set a baseline for what constitutes an active user in terms of volume, then you can group these and say, "We have 100 active users who engaged with content in the last month." We'll talk more about how to create these baselines and categories of users in Chapter 14, and you can see an example of what measuring consumption might look like in Figure 12.2.

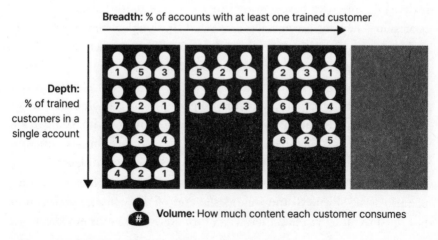

Figure 12.2 Measuring Content Consumption

Level One: Reaction

Once you've looked at Engagement, the next thing to evaluate is Reaction. Ask yourself, did your learners enjoy the training? The data you can collect here can be as simple as upvotes and downvotes, smile sheets, five-point scales, or CSAT and NPS scores. You'll also be looking at completion rate, because on a simple level if users completed your course, that's a pretty good signal that they thought it was worth their time. Completion rate is also a simple metric that your LMS is likely to offer without too much work on your side.

However, we would caution that completion rate isn't a metric on which to hang the success of your program. As it's one of the most common metrics used in the customer education world, let's zoom in on completion rate in more detail. Your goal is to get as close as possible to 100 percent, so that you can see everyone who starts your course has finished it. According to Massive Online Open Courses (MOOCs) data, completion rate tends to fall between 5 and 15 percent.[2]

In our experience with customer education, we would estimate that it's more like 40 percent. Intuitively, that makes a lot of sense, as MOOC is usually longer content, less exciting, or engaging, and not always aligned with what the learner wants. A person might choose to learn SQL or project management or public speaking in their own time and then drop out when it's not what they expect. In the customer education world, your audience includes people who have already invested in the product and want to be successful. They are intrinsically motivated to complete the course, as it's tied to drivers like their own achievement and work satisfaction.

However, the reason why course completion isn't a defining metric is that it's fairly easy to manipulate. If you have an hour-long course where your learners regularly drop out after 40 percent, you could break it down into 10 parts, and suddenly you have four mini-courses with 100 percent completion rates. You can also choose to define completion rate on your own terms by using your LMS. Has the course been completed as soon as learners open the page, or when they start the final video? Do they need to scroll down all the way to the end of the content, or can they just open the final page? If they skip a formative quiz in the middle, is the

---

[2] Katy Jordan, *MOOC Completion Rates: The Data* (eLearning and Innovative Pedagogies, 2013).

course incomplete? Because of these key questions, it's easy for companies to define completion criteria with the goal in mind of driving up completion rates.

The only noticeably helpful way to use completion rates is when measuring the impact of a change to content. If you're keeping all of your completion criteria the same – and you aren't breaking down the content in any way – you can change elements of your content, such as streamlining a moment of friction and then measuring the impact of your edits on completion.

Level Two: Learning

The best way to measure whether learning has taken place is using summative assessments. Think about any activity at the end of a course, from quizzes to self-reflection activities, and these can give you a good idea of whether learning has taken place. In some cases, you can create something more formal, such as a certification. This will signal to the business, the customer, and more widely the market that the learning has taken place. Of course it doesn't guarantee any kind of application of this learning – it just means the customer has gained some mastery of the material (assuming the certification exam is effectively measuring learning transference). Many companies evaluate whether their customer base has sufficient product knowledge by measuring the percentage of customers to have earned the certification.

Level Three: Behavior

Behavior is also an impact metric, and to analyze this you'll need to look at what your goals were to begin with all the way back in Step 1. If you were looking to teach customers how to get started using the product, then you'll be measuring TTV (time to value). If you wanted users to learn how to use a particular feature, on the other hand, product adoption will be your key metric.

At this point, a lot of programs reach their maximum level of sophistication. Using cohort analysis of trained versus nontrained customers, you can use this data to really understand the success of your education, discovering what TTV or product adoption looks like for accounts with 10 people trained, 50 people trained, or no one trained at all. These are powerful correlations to draw.

Level Four: Results

Continuing with our impact metrics, we can turn to more strategic ways to measure success. In the Kirkpatrick model, next we look at whether the change in customer behavior had an impact on the business. Sometimes you teach your customers something and it impacts their behavior, but that doesn't carry over to an impact on the business. In that case, you may need to take a step back and ask if that behavioral change is important. If your education results in increased feature adoption just as you were hoping for, but it doesn't impact the number of subscription renewals, what you've learned is that perhaps the feature isn't where you should focus your efforts! This is valuable insight to take back to your product team, that the feature isn't so important to your customers.

If you have the technology and the infrastructure to run A/B testing, these can be very powerful to help get more insight into deeper customer behavior. An example to measure the impact of training on retention would be taking a number of accounts that are in the "yellow zone" – in danger of churning but not about to churn imminently – and randomly selecting half to be offered a free training session. By tracking all the yellow accounts over the next few months, you can measure the impact of the training.

Another example for product engagement would be a test we performed at Optimizely, where we created an in-product educational guider delivered through Pendo. We didn't give the control group the guider, and 13 percent of the group engaged with a specific feature on their own. The other half got the guider, and the percentage rose to 51 percent. This gave us a clear causal connection between the education and the adoption of the feature.

In many cases, the minutiae of causal impact won't affect your business bottom line. Instead, it's important to think about the bigger picture. The ideal customer is one who gets value, renews, and expands their usage. If you look at common behaviors of these ideal customers – you'll probably find engaging with training content is high up on the list. If you're looking to create a strategy to support the ideal customer, you want them to be engaging with training.

One of the most notable enhancements to the Kirkpatrick model came from Jack Phillips, the founder of the ROI Institute. He added a fifth level, ROI, to look at business outcomes and to compare the benefits of lead generation, retention, increased NPS score, and more with the costs of running the program.[3] We'll talk more about ROI and how to internally tell the story of your success in Chapter 15.

Prioritizing and Focusing on the Right Data

After creating your data dictionary with all the relevant information included – you might be starting to notice that overwhelming feeling we talked about earlier. What are the right data points to track to understand the impact of the education on your customer? Do you want to show behavioral change, learning, impact on their business, or something else entirely? Now's the time to prioritize the data you'll use to assess the success of your education. Don't worry – you should have already done a lot of the work to answer these questions. Look back at the first few steps of the *Playbook*, and ask yourself:

- **How do your customers define success?** This forces us to put ourselves in our customers' shoes. Think back to Step 2 where you outlined how to make your customers' jobs easier through added knowledge, efficiency, or accuracy. If you were looking to improve the customer experience, CSATs would be a good choice, while if you were hoping to speed up onboarding, then you might choose to use your customer support ticket data.
- **Did your customers learn what they needed to know?** Here's where we answer the "so what?" Your customers might have completed your course, passed an assessment, given you a high smile score, or added a certification to their belt – but what were you hoping to achieve by their learning? Did they adopt a particular feature, reach their TTV faster, or engage with upsell opportunities?

---

[3] Jack J. Phillips, *Return on Investment in Training and Performance Improvement Programs,* 2nd ed. (Butterworth-Heinemann, 2003).

With these three steps in mind, you should be able to isolate a key result, or perhaps two or three metrics that you want to drive. You can then use your data dictionary and the rest of your operational dashboard to help you to triangulate and identify opportunities for future educational initiatives.

Communicating the Success of the Education Back to the Customer

One step that is often missed but can be really valuable is to report your findings about the success of the education back to the customer themselves. When your customer completes a course, look to add delightful moments where you throw some confetti over the screen, send them a certificate, or award them some kind of milestone achievement badge. If you don't have an LMS dashboard, send them a monthly email that celebrates how much learning they have taken, listing what they've done really well and encouraging them into the next stage of their education.

You can also use your wider customer data to help learners understand their relationship to your education, and to tap into social proof – the way that people are heavily influenced by what other people are doing. Try something like, "You've spent 25 hours on this training – the average customer spends 30 hours, or 15 hours." Add data points like "Customers who complete this training are 50 percent more likely to find value in the first 90 days of using the product." You're handing over information about how they can get ROI faster from your product, and giving a measurable way for them to answer the "WIIFM?".

The way that you measure and assess the success of your customer education will also change as your customer base and your education function grows. Tom Studdert at ZoomInfo has a large customer education function, with 50 employees working in his team. He provides his insight below on how ZoomInfo uses their own adapted Kirkpatrick model as a foundation to measure success at scale.

Thoughts from . . . Tom Studdert, Vice President of Customer Onboarding and Implementations, ZoomInfo

Every company will be at a different place in how they assess and measure education. When we first started our customer learning and development team at ZoomInfo, we were barely tracking whether people showed up to our training. Today, we have five levels of measurement. If you had asked me what I wanted more data on six years ago, I would have been happy to know who was participating in what we were putting out there. Even a year ago, I would have said it would be great to get a better grasp on how our training was impacting the rest of the business. Today, I'd love to find a more quantitative way to measure the impact of our training on the customer's own business metrics without interviewing 25,000 customers individually! These goals take time.

If you're less mature as a function, it's fine to be working on your level of sophistication – just keep your eye on where you want to get to, and start measuring.

Looking at Learning Outcomes and Success

Customer education can be an optional activity for your audience, so measuring that you're getting eyes on your content and making an impact is really important. I like to align the metrics we track with an adapted version of the Kirkpatrick model, expanded to five levels. We use a pyramid of metrics (Figure 12.3), starting with foundational metrics of participation, satisfaction, and engagement, moving up to our business metrics of usage and impact. We measure this across individuals, accounts, and also by customer size and segment. While I am more focused on the aggregate top-line numbers, our customer learning and development managers are measured by their impact on individual users and accounts.

(continued)

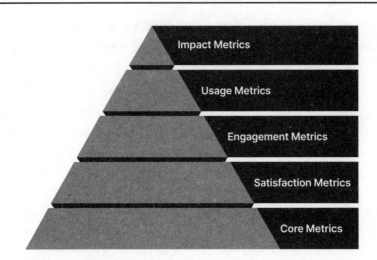

Figure 12.3 Zoominfo Pyramid of Metrics

Of course, we want to improve everything on the pyramid. You can't isolate the metrics at the apex without the others that live further down.

Some are more difficult to draw a direct line from in terms of results. Satisfaction, for example, can be a tricky one, as only a certain percentage of your learners want to give a star rating or fill out a smile sheet on their way out of training, which immediately skews the data to those who want to provide feedback. I do love getting and incorporating immediate reactions from the learners, such as emails to the trainer after a session or an ad-hoc comment in the Zoom chat, but generally speaking, you can take the satisfaction metric with a grain of salt.

Once we get there, the most important goals to us are usage and impact. Usage looks at whether customers interact with the feature or product to a greater extent, and impact dives deeper to see whether we've affected behavioral change, which is our ultimate goal.

Training = Retaining

When the Customer Experience team at ZoomInfo is formed, we work with an outside partner to identify the key features within our platform that would help customers see value with the product, and therefore make it more likely that they would retain. We measure effectiveness by our ability to get customers to use these features, knowing that if the education function can achieve increased usage, the business will see that impact on retention. We run reports daily to track the impact of our training on usage with that goal in mind.

Of course, it's not just about whether customers are using the platform and coming back, although that's a great start. It's about whether they are using the product in the way that they have been taught – whether behavioral change has occurred.

Let's say a customer has attended training about how to use advanced search. The next time they log in, we look at whether they interact with advanced search, but also we ask, do they filter the way that they have been taught, and generally use advanced search the way that the training laid it out? Each piece of educational content, whether it's a video, an on-demand course or a certification, has a learning outcome that aligns with a specific impact metric, trying to get the customer to do something in a new way. This is the impact of the education, and it relates to a customer goal as well as an underlying business goal. Continuing with the same example, the learning outcome for the customer might be to use advanced search to find what they need quicker or with greater accuracy, while for the business, we may be looking to increase advanced search usage month over month to deepen product adoption or reduce churn. We want to tie a direct line from our educational efforts to the customer's use case for bringing on Zoom Info, which will in turn help create our own direct line from customer usage to business impact.

Focusing on the Customer Need

The starting point for determining whether education is successful is therefore understanding what the customer is looking to gain.

(continued)

That's a conversation we have with the customer during onboarding, sometimes involving pre-education that helps them to figure out how to get from what they think they want to what they actually need. While we certainly have standardized tracks, every training is different to meet the goals and KPIs that the customer is looking to measure and achieve.

As we've scaled, we've had to find new ways to make this happen. We now have 25,000 customers and 250,000 end users. An open invite to a live Zoom isn't going to cut it! We've created what I call the "Choose your own adventure model." Based on needs and timeline, customers can choose the education that they want to consume. We host live webinars every day on foundational topics like onboarding, and we can provide a customized training video in our university within five days for a specific customer on request. If the customer can wait two weeks and wants something more interactive, we can deliver live training. If they're in more of a hurry, they could sign up to become a customer on Monday and go to a webinar later that day to hit the ground running.

Once you have come to grips with some data around how your customers are learning, and you're starting to see where content is hitting the mark or falling short, you can look for ways to iterate and improve on what you've built so far. We'll provide some ideas and best practices for enhancing and improving existing content in the next chapter.

13

Step 11: Actionable Strategies to Improve Your Content

Once you've published your content and successfully measured its impact, it can be tempting to report your findings, then get straight to your next project. However, this is a missed opportunity. It's really valuable at this stage to take the time to explore how your content can be improved.

If you look back on how you chose to measure the success of your education in Step 10, these metrics become your signals for which content is performing well and which is doing poorly. In this chapter, we will explore how to improve the content that isn't hitting its mark.

Understanding Iterative Design

Improving content requires a real commitment to the idea of iteration. Mark it out forcibly as an item on the to-do list, create a motivated team for it, and put a meeting in your calendars where the agenda is iterating and improving content. Treat your projects like they are living things – you must nurture them, check in regularly, improve and maintain them – rather than just build and forget.

Your iteration mindset should start immediately, right from the idea-tion stage. Think about the content that you want to create, and continu-ously aim to validate your assumptions, looking at any data you can use to make improvements even before your education is ready to go live. Invite other stakeholders to whiteboarding sessions or meetings where you can get some feedback on small or large changes, and thoughts about how it alters the flow or the feel of the experience. If you're truly adopting an iterative mindset, you're thinking, "How can I improve from day one?" not waiting for the content to be in the wild before you consider tweaks and changes. Make sure you also have a system set up to manage content after it goes live, so that you can keep it up to date as the product evolves and changes – updating screen grabs, adding features, or changing messaging where necessary.

Look at the Feedback

Sometimes when you're in the process of improving your education, you'll realize that you're shooting from the hip more than you'd like, relying on gut instinct rather than data. While this intuition can come from deep expe-rience and theoretical knowledge, your hypotheses need to be backed up with explicit data sources. Part of improving education is to look for places to collect these signals on what to improve in the first place. If you don't have a way to validate your assumptions, you may need to add additional feedback loops where you ask the learner, "How did you like this training?" or insert a pop-up near the beginning with a simple thumbs up or down interface and the prompt "How are we doing so far?"

Quantitative feedback such as a rating from 1 to 5 or an upvote/ downvote system is great, but you also need qualitative explicit data streams. Open-ended feedback is often the richest data and can be incred-ibly helpful during your iteration meetings. Learners will openly provide you with ways to improve, such as, "I wish the course had covered X topic," or, "That quiz was way too hard." This can be a real gift. This kind of feedback is easy to collect without devoting huge amounts of time or effort, often by simply showing up at a meeting where multiple customers are in attendance.

Don't be tempted to dismiss feedback that you hear only once. First, chances are that the feedback also represents the feelings of silent voices. Second, you can use this data triangulated with quantitative data or your own hypothesis to come up with powerful changes. If a single person says a video is too long, and you see that it has the lowest completion rates, for example – that's a pretty good sign that you need to cut it down or break it up.

Sometimes you'll get contradictory feedback, such as five people saying a course was too easy, and another five saying it was too hard. This is informative in itself! The improvement you want to make in this kind of scenario is being clearer about the optimal skill level of the education. Go back to the registration page and manage expectations or add clarity for your learners as to whether this is the right course for their needs. In this situation, you might also find that your course is uneven in its approach. See if you can pull it apart and create something basic and something advanced out of the existing content, separating it for the two audiences.

Improving Support Content

Your first step when you're looking to iterate and improve the content in knowledge bases or help documentation is to find data that helps you identify gaps. You want to find the questions that keep coming up about a given topic where there aren't resources in place to provide clear answers. One option is to use search data and see what common terms your customers are looking for in multiple ways, since this suggests that they aren't finding what they need. Either you don't have the right content, or it isn't discoverable enough. Perhaps you had put content in place, but it's out of date, needs a refresh, or it has been changed or removed.

Daniel on Using Search Queries to Identify Content Gaps

At Asana, I'd get a report every month of the top search terms our customers used. At one stage, I kept seeing the search term "tags" pop up, and after the third time I did an audit and realized there wasn't any content around tags. After I spoke to product marketing, I found that it was a purposeful strategy to encourage people to use a new feature – custom fields – and move away from using tags. Unfortunately, by making that change, we had actually created friction for customers. We still offered tags in the product, and there were very nuanced ways that customers were using tagging to inform and deepen their use of the product, but there was no content around how to use it. Tracking search queries and identifying patterns can be a quick and easy way to identify content gaps!

Another way to find places to enhance education is to look at the questions that your support team are fielding. If at the end of training, you're getting multiple users asking the same question, then that's a pretty clear sign that there's a topic missing that needs to be incorporated into the training itself. If there are support tickets where the customer success team can't attach articles or resources to bolster their response, or where the customer comes back again and asks another question – this is a gap that needs to be filled. Remember, no one wants to go to support, so your goal is to resolve tickets in a single interaction, allowing your customers to get back to doing their job. If that isn't happening, then the resource is failing.

How Do You Know If Help Articles Have Been Successful?

One way to demonstrate how successful your help articles are is to look at your web analytics and see which visitors left your knowledge base immediately after reading one article. You can also watch average time on the knowledge base; decrease over time is a good sign. The goal of your knowledge base isn't to keep people hanging around, whiling away an afternoon exploring all of your help articles. That's the role of your academy, to make people excited and involved in learning. In your help center, if you see that customers read one article, then head back to the search box to look up a related term or click on additional help articles under the original, your content has not been successful. In contrast, if customers immediately bounce after reading the article, this is a pretty good indication that they've found what they needed.

Using the Help Content Optimization Matrix to Visualize How to Improve Support Content

One approach for understanding how to improve help articles was first surfaced by Adam Avramescu in his book, *Customer Education, Why Smart Companies Profit by Making Customers Smarter*.[1] Named in Figure 13.1 as the Help Content Optimization Matrix, it can be incredibly useful. In fact, once you start using it, you might find that you refer to it regularly!

On the matrix are four quadrants. On the *x*-axis, you mark how discoverable an article is by how much traffic it has seen. On the *y*-axis, you

Figure 13.1 Help Content Optimization Matrix

---

[1] Adam Avramescu, *Customer Education, Why Smart Companies Profit by Making Customers Smarter* (Adam Avramescu © 2019).

mark the percentage of customers who indicated that it was helpful, the ratio between the thumbs-up and thumbs-down ratings.

Once you've plotted your articles on the matrix, in the top right you'll see articles that both get a lot of traffic and your customers find helpful. These are your core, crucial, most valuable articles. Leverage these! Repurpose them into additional training experiences, protect them, and iterate them where necessary with new screenshots or updated information to keep them highly relevant.

In the bottom-right corner, you'll have content that is getting a lot of eyes on it, but isn't helpful enough. This would indicate that it should be high on the priority list to improve. Can you make it clearer, add images, or make it more accurate?

In the top-left corner, the content is helpful, but has low traffic. This is valuable content that customers aren't finding! This could be because it's a niche feature, but it could also be that you need to fix some SEO problems with the page or feature the article by sending it out in an email or highlighting in-product. Consider promoting these articles.

Finally, in the lower-left corner you'll have content that isn't helpful and gets little engagement. Don't get attached to content just because it exists. If it isn't getting traffic and your customers aren't finding it helpful – perhaps it's time to delete or archive it.

An alternate approach for using the matrix is to replace the helpfulness ratio with the bounce rate metric that we discussed above. For many, this might be a more objective way of measuring helpfulness, as upvoting and downvoting can be conflated with emotions around the content. A customer could mark an article as unhelpful because it explains that the product can't do a particular task that they were looking to achieve, or because it informs them that the feature they need is a premium add-on. However, if they leave immediately, it was still successful at providing the answer they were looking for.

Improving Training Content

Unlike support content, which is optimized for troubleshooting, training content is designed for learning. You'll need to track different metrics to measure the success of training content and work out where to iterate and improve.

Improving Consumption

Two common ways to measure content consumption are enrollment and completion rates. First, check your distribution strategy, as we discussed in Step 9. Make sure you're working with marketing, support, and customer success teams to drive consumption of content. If you're using a platform like Thought Industries, you'll have the customer's email address and can also leverage in-LMS notifications. Send reminders to nudge them to continue their learning journey or to complete an unfinished course. You can also set up a button on the home page that helps learners pick up where they left off.

Once you've ensured you have a sound consumption strategy, you'll want to explore tactics for improving the content itself. I have found some tactics particularly helpful in improving enrollment and completion.

Change Your Titles   No one is trained by the title of your course, so your headings aren't educational content. Instead, think of your titles as small pieces of marketing content. They are a signal to the market of the value that customers will get from taking your course and why they should care. Your titles and your subtitles should grab your customer, get them to enroll, and then continue through to complete the whole course.

Daniel on the Importance of Active Titles

In one of my iteration meetings, we formed a hypothesis, based on enrollment and completion rates, that the titles of our lessons were too boring. We changed the titles of the course to speak more directly to customer outcomes and value. Instead of a passive title like "Choosing an audience," we added questions and made them a lot more active, such as "How do I target my experiment to a specific audience?" It made a huge difference and led to a significant increase in engagement with those lessons.

Check Your Registration Pages   Have you ever noticed how poorly designed landing pages for course registrations can be? They often have too much text, way too little text, or a dry or boring explanation. A well-designed course detail page is a marketing project and requires you to think, "What can I do to make this compelling?" Look to show value immediately and encourage people to join. Use images, play with colors, and highlight text to draw learners in. One impactful idea is to use talking heads here, including a very short, 30-second video that compels people to press the play button and gets them invested in the content before they've even signed up.

Funnel Analysis   If the issue isn't enrollment but completion rates, then a funnel analysis can be really helpful, as shown in Figure 13.2. This is where you take the number of people that enrolled, then mark the people who finished each lesson, all the way through to completion of the whole course. You'll be able to visualize a funnel that shows where people drop out. It's

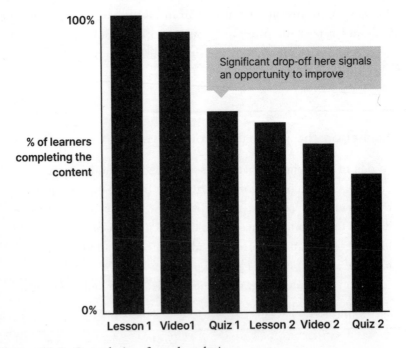

Figure 13.2 Completion funnel analysis

unrealistic to expect a flat line to completion, but sometimes you'll have a smooth line to the end, which is great as long as it isn't too steep. Other times, such as in the previous example, you'll see steep drop-off points, and then you can target completion for a specific lesson. You could reduce the specific video length, cut the number of questions in a quiz, or add a formative experience that keeps users engaged.

Consider Your Monetization Strategy   We talked back in Step 9 about how to charge for your content, and it might be that after market analysis, you realize that you've overproduced content that isn't meeting demand. You have a few options here. You can recalibrate the price to meet the market or offer discounts to incentivize learners. You can also bundle the content with other courses to try to get consumption rates up. It might also be worth amping up the perceived value. Add an expert interview, access to instructors, or some additional job aids that will show your learners what's in it for them.

Improving Customer Satisfaction Rates

If your goal is to improve your CSAT scores, have a picture in mind for what improvement looks like. Let's say you want a score of 4.0, and you're looking to improve that baseline by increments of 0.20 over time. Think strategically and make sure to lean on the explicit data that you've collected. This section discusses tips for improving CSAT scores by leveraging data.

Collect Feedback   As we discussed above, it's essential to create explicit feedback loops if your goal is to improve customer satisfaction. We recommend creating a survey that your customers fill out at the end of a learning experience. Instead of sending the survey once the course has been completed, it can help to increase engagement with the survey to offer it right after the lesson, but before the Certificate of Completion. You can even make the call-to-action for submitting the survey "Complete Course." Add a handful of questions to this survey, but keep it fewer than five. Ask about overall satisfaction, perceived difficulty, engagement (the "fun" factor), relevance to the persona, and whether the course met the learner's expectations on what they hoped to learn. Make sure to include an open-ended field (e.g., "How would you suggest we improve the course?") Responses to these types of questions can be gold!

Organize Feedback   Look for themes and patterns, such as engagement, comprehensiveness, helpfulness, or user experience. Make sure to have a process in place to track this information over time, rather than looking at each iteration in a silo. This will help to gather more "big picture" information, as well as help you understand how a change you made affected customer sentiment.

Prioritize Feedback   Note whether feedback is objective or subjective. Prioritize objective feedback first, such as "There's a typo in slide 4!" This is the easiest feedback to fix. With objective feedback, think about whether the changes will be quick or lengthy, and cross-reference that by the impact of the change. If the feedback you get is that a customer doesn't like the color scheme of the course, or they've taken issue with one of the animated characters, this might take a lot of time and effort to fix, and ultimately it won't affect the learning, so you might decide to ignore such subjective comments altogether.

Use Your Experience and Insight   Ask yourself, "What do my customers not know about their own reactions to training that they don't realize they don't know?" Often, customers won't put into words what the real problem is. They might say, "It's boring." If you're a learning experience designer, you can probably list in your sleep the reasons why learning content isn't engaging. While the customer didn't say explicitly that the content is too dense, all text, or lacks interactivity, these are problems you can look for, putting the right strategies in place in response to what you find.

Improving Certifications

For certifications, it's less relevant whether your customers are satisfied. After all, no one likes a tough test, but when you are granting someone a certification that signals to the market a certain level of mastery in a field, sometimes a tough test is exactly what they need. If you've built a certification, you should have someone on board who understands psychometrics and can help you to use item analysis to improve your certification where necessary.

Make Questions Hard, but Not Too Hard

The overall goal for certification improvement is to ensure that it has the right balance and isn't too hard or too easy for your learners. To get a feel for this, you'll want to drill down to each item on the test and analyze it to understand how good a question it is. An ideal question will correctly discriminate between those who know the topic well enough to gain the certification and those who don't. If 100 percent of people got that question correct, it's essentially a useless question and the distractors – the incorrect answers – aren't doing their job. Similarly, if 0 percent of people got the question right, your distractors are pulling in those with a higher aptitude, which is equally problematic. You can also look at how much time people are spending on each question – no more than a minute per question is best practice.

There Is Such Thing as a Bad Question

Writing questions for professional credentials like certifications is an expert skill, and should have the goal of effectively separating your low performers and high performers to establish who has true expertise. Whatever questions you choose, make sure to validate these with professionals who you deem to be experts in doing that job. You want to hear from these experts that you've chosen great questions that only someone with their level of expertise would be able to answer. Check your questions for clarity and accuracy, ensure that all answers are a consistent length, and avoid pitfalls such as double-barreled questions (i.e., a question that addresses more than one issue but only allows for one answer), "all of the above/none of the above" options, and the use of true/false.

Knowing When to Archive Content

Remember, sometimes removing content altogether is the best choice that you can make to improve your education. It's easy to fall into the sunk-cost fallacy, where you think about all the time and effort you spent on education and get too focused on improving or updating content that really isn't giving the customer any value. If the content doesn't have potential, you're just throwing your time and resources away. Cleaning house is a sound and rational decision, and if you can see from your data streams that the content isn't useful, there is no value to it filling up your course page, help center, or academy.

Cary Self is the global vice president of Education and Program Development at CustomerGauge. He shares his thoughts below on how to improve and iterate customer education.

Thoughts from . . . Cary Self, Global Vice President of Education and Program Development at CustomerGauge

When I started at CustomerGauge, I was tasked with improving and updating the customer education right out of the gate. I started by looking at the metrics we had around content consumption. What were learners consuming, and what were they completing? I found that the drop-off rate was around 70 or 80 percent. Pretty dire, and usually an indication that your content is either god-awful boring or badly targeted. Senior sponsors were tuning out, managers were losing interest . . . something wasn't working.

The next step was to get some feedback. We found two groups of users. One said that the courses were too long and slow, and the other said the content wasn't tactical enough for their needs. Once we had that feedback, the actual solutions were simple. We broke the content up into smaller pieces, which gave people a feeling of greater accomplishment as they finished a section and moved onto the next. We also used this feedback to realize we were missing a lot of the "chips in the cookie," the practical and helpful stuff that makes a course worthwhile. There was no need to reinvent the wheel. We already had a ton of content, it just wasn't in our education. We had videos from events, case studies with our customers, office hour webinars . . . all we needed to do was bring it together. We went from 30 percent completion rates to between 80 and 90 percent completion rates. Not only that, but learners were more engaged, finishing a course in two weeks that traditionally took multiple months, asking more questions, and moving on to consume additional content after the courses were complete. I even had a customer say, "Customer-Gauge Academy is my new Netflix!"

Considering the Environment

Sometimes it's not the education itself that needs tweaking. I've found that the environment itself can be a sticking point. Our content used to be on a white screen with dark letters, and we found that people were getting fatigued. I thought back to my college days when I was studying in a dorm room late at night. Everyone remembers dimming the screen as low as possible. We wanted to create an experience that makes you want to keep going. We now use Night mode inside the Academy, and we've found that learners stay on average 30–40 minutes longer. We mobile-optimized our Academy and started offering our education on the go, and suddenly people are working outside of the 9–5, because it's easier to consume out of the office.

Other changes you can trial relate to the bigger picture, such as your business model. We hypothesized that people who pay for content have more skin in the game, so we monetized the education, not to make money, as a lot of the costs of our education are baked into the subscription price anyway, but because people who invest in themselves have a greater tendency to see a course or a certification through to completion. We also added tiers of content, thinking about audience personas and creating a sleek and streamlined version for the C-suite and a more technical version for managers.

Creating a Healthy Feedback Channel

Learners can often be our best editors. We have a connected survey system that allows customers to provide feedback when they finish a course or a certification. At CustomerGauge we look to mirror the

(continued)

customer experience with the employee experience, and glean feedback from both channels simultaneously. For example, we ask new employees to do the same onboarding training that we offer to new customers. Onboarding used to take 60–90 days, but our training has reduced that to 2–4 weeks. In under 30 days, we can now set up a whole campaign and get customers into the system using the platform. As employees take the same training, that means that within 30 days, they are also fully versed in how to use the platform, with the same language that the customers are using. We often see them becoming almost brand ambassadors for education – they've taken the training and seen how valuable it can be, so when a customer comes with a new query, they might say "We could create a course for that!" They know that what they can teach in an hour to five or six people in an account manually could reach tens of thousands with the right on-demand content.

Getting employees involved is an important part of the process of improving the content for me. I won't hand something to the customer if my team hasn't completed it first. I usually ask a small group of customers or employees to experience the learning first before putting it into the wild. For a customer, I might offer to waive the fee for training as an incentive in return for some feedback. We'll get a lot of qualitative feedback from this of course, and we'll also uncover quantitative information, like if everyone gets a specific question wrong in a quiz then we know we've either taught the concept badly or asked the question badly! We have ongoing workshops and meetings where we feed all of the improvements we get back into the content itself. We're never looking to revamp and improve a whole program in one shot – it's a modular and iterative process, which also helps to keep people engaged in providing the feedback we need.

I try to switch things up with who I invite to give feedback so I don't get all the same kind of users. I'll speak to senior sponsors, admin users, internal people from sales or support. Maybe I'll ask a customer who hasn't ever touched educational content before, or a colleague who is a bit of a resistor, and isn't bought into the idea of the training in the first place. I challenge them, "Tell me why this isn't going to work!"

Remove the Emotional Attachment You Have to Your Content

Being a content creator, and being the one who is receiving the feedback, it can be easy to become protective over the education. Try to take any emotion out of the process, and remember that there is no such thing as bad feedback. Sometimes you might hear overwhelmingly that the content isn't hitting the mark, and you need to archive it – or salvage some nuggets and put it behind you. Other times, you might get a single piece of negative feedback, and you need to understand whether it's one brave person who's telling you what you need to hear or just a detractor or an attention-seeker, or someone who has ended up in the wrong training that doesn't suit their needs. After all, people learn in different ways. Some people want to be interactive, some want to share and collaborate, and some just want to read. Look to the metrics and see if they agree with the feedback you're getting. If someone says the content is boring, are the completion rates low? Does it seem longer than it should be? There could well be value in what they are saying. Take it to a feedback group or to the rest of your team and ask, "What do you think of this feedback we got?"

Then, remember to acknowledge it. Thank the learner for their feedback and close the loop by explaining what your decision was on next steps, even if that's just the knowledge that you fed back their thoughts to the rest of the team. As a company, that helps other organizations measure the voice of the customer, I can tell you that you never want to discourage that voice from speaking up.

Taking an iterative approach to the customer education that you create means opening up channels for feedback, looking hard at the data to see what needs to be changed or included, and aligning your improvement strategies with the type of content that you're providing. Once you're sure that your content is hitting its mark, it's time to demonstrate the impact of the education and show the value of what you've done so that you can grow your program with additional investment.

14

Step 12: Demonstrate the ROI of Customer Education

Ultimately, everything that you've done so far, from creating the right education to meet your goals and engage the learner to distributing, measuring, and iterating content, needs to lead to a place where you can prove the worth of your customer education program according to business impact.

We mentioned back in Step 10 (Chapter 12) that teams often struggle to measure the success of their education, and we talked about measuring the impact of your program on customer consumption and satisfaction. But measuring success is about much more than getting a handle on who is consuming content and who isn't (although that's important, of course). It's about getting the right people to buy into your story. The bottom line is, if you can't draw a connection from the customer education function to the rest of the business, how can you make a case for greater investment to grow your team or expand your portfolio? Ultimately, if your data exists in a vacuum, how will you get a seat at the proverbial table and help to drive strategy for the business at large?

Without data to back up the ROI you're providing, you have to rely on executives just "getting it," – coming to you and saying, "I don't need to see the proof of your impact, I understand the underlying value of customers learning and being trained and how it relates to our success." Even if you're lucky enough to have an executive sponsor who "gets it," don't get complacent! Relying on this kind of buy-in alone isn't enough. If we want a seat at the table, we should hold ourselves to the same standards that other departments hold themselves to, and look for data-driven signals around the impact of the work we're doing.

Collecting the Data to Measure Business Impact

The first thing you want to think about is how you're going to connect your education data to other systems and objectives across the organization. Ideally, you want to be able to compare and analyze cross-departmental data, so that you can understand the impact of trained and non-trained users on data, including support tickets, renewals, churn, and lead generation. While it's possible to collect this information manually, it's going to be tough to do these kinds of analyses without connecting your data to other systems. If your company has a data warehouse with a business intelligence tool to visualize data, make it a priority to hook up your own data!

The Formula for ROI

Especially if you're running a profit center, it's really important to be able to work out the monetary ROI of your education program. Here is a quick formula that you can use. Take the monetary benefits, subtract your training costs, then divide by the training costs and multiply this number to get a percentage. Let's say your program made $100,000, and cost $25,000 to make. 100k – 25k = 75k. 75k divided by 25k = 3. Multiplied by 100, that means your ROI is 300 percent.

Start by working out your training costs, which is often the easy part. This is usually split into three main categories: the headcount of your team, the technology you're using, and your contractors. Add up the salaries in your department, the annual contract value for the technology that is primarily used by the education team, and the costs of any contractors that you use for writing, training delivery, or any other ad-hoc function, and you should have a pretty clear idea of your costs.

Monetary benefits are trickier. If you have decided to create a direct revenue stream and you have a fee-based strategy, then you've got an easy number to use – your direct sales. Some companies who have robust education services, and who make millions of dollars a year in direct revenue will stop here. They simply subtract the costs from the revenue, and that's what they're held to in terms of ROI. However, most customer education programs have goals that indirectly impact revenue. While these programs may have some kind of fee-based training, they are largely cost centers or cost recovery centers. That means that there won't be enough direct sales revenue to compensate for training costs.

Moreover, we know that monetary benefits aren't the only benefits. The impact of education is on product adoption, renewals, ticket deflection, and more. Your ability to measure these, and to put a monetary value on them, will help you to prove the ROI of your education, even if it doesn't garner direct sales or revenues.

Using a Training Score to Create a Cohort Analysis

In Step 10 (Chapter 12), we touched on using categories of users to better understand the relationship between training and other metrics in the business. We talked about using active, underactive, and inactive categories for your accounts, although you could also use highly trained, trained, and untrained – or whatever labels work for you. Essentially, you're giving every account a score, 1, 2, or 3, in line with these categories. You get to decide how to define the categories. Some companies consider accounts who engage with free content to be level 2, and you need to pay for content to reach level 3. Others will use quantity, so zero courses versus one course versus five courses to move through the rankings. We like using certifications, so highly trained accounts are those where they have earned at least one certification. The point is that you have a scoring system and you stick to it consistently.

To use this data effectively, we're going to go back to our old friend cohort analysis. You'll need to access other metrics in the organization such as new sales, customers who have expanded their usage, or support tickets across accounts. You then take the training scores and measure the accounts by their categories, looking at their average rates for expansion, adoption, support tickets, or churn.

Let's think about measuring support deflection as an example. Of all the accounts who filed support tickets, how many were highly trained accounts? If you can see that 3s are filing far fewer support tickets than 0s, and you know that the average cost of a support ticket for your organization is $15.56, you now have a way to put a monetary value on the impact of your education. (Speak to your support managers if you're looking for a number to use for the cost of your support tickets, they should be able to help.)

Don't stop there! Are 1s churning more than 3s? Do 2s have a higher rate of renewal than 1s? Are your 1s taking longer to get to value with your product than any other group? With each metric, you're beginning to form the ability to tell a really good story about ROI for your program.

Even if you don't have the data analysis tools, do an ad-hoc analysis. Manually take a slice of data from Salesforce or wherever the information you need is stored and create the same cohort analysis. It will certainly take longer, and you'll be capturing a moment in time rather than accessing a continuous feed of data, but in a pinch, it works!

Daniel on Correlation versus Causation

I used to be of the mindset that causation was the standard that all of us should be pursuing in our education programs. I have a product background, and running experiments is bread and butter to me. However, as it turns out, it's really hard to run statistically significant experiments to prove a causal relationship with training! Usually there aren't enough users, or there are too many systems at play, so you can't control the experiment adequately. There's also a challenge with a lack of a control group, as it isn't in your interests to deliberately withhold training from your customers and then watch with an interested face to see if they churn. Even if you promote training to one group and not another, this only provides insight into the offer of training, not the impact of the training itself. While you might find evidence that trained customers are far more likely to be retained, the truth is that if your customers are unhappy with your product for any number of reasons, then they are far less likely to enroll in a training course. Conversely, your customers who are using the product and finding it valuable with no training at all are more likely to go looking for a course to deepen their mastery. In short, it's hard to parse the signal from the noise.

As a result, over time I've backed down from the idea that running causal studies was necessary to prove the impact of customer education. I accept the underlying premise that learning is important, which is pretty hard to refute, and I'm okay with not knowing whether correlation is causation when I look at my data.

Let's say, for example, that using the method above, I find a high correlation between training and renewal rates. It's true that I don't know whether it's because trained customers are more likely to renew or because those same customers who are likely to renew are also more likely to engage with training. The direction of the relationship is unclear, but that's okay. Either training is causing these customers to renew – in which case, awesome, let's keep it up – or the customers who are most likely to renew are the ones who engage with training. In that case, completing training is an important quality of a customer who renews – so it's important to invest in customer learning programs.

Telling the Story of Your Impact

Once you've collected the data that correlates your training to other areas of the business, and translated this into ROI, you're ready to tell your story to others. Communication skills are just as important (if not more important) than the technical data you've collected.

If the idea of giving the presentation and effectively explaining your value makes you feel stressed, remember that you already work in designing learning experiences, and this really shouldn't be any different from that! Don't get hung up on the idea of "I have to make this complex presentation in order to convince people to give me more funding." You have expertise in designing learning experiences, so take a step back and ask yourself, what does your audience (in this case, your leadership team) need to learn? Your job here is to design something that will effectively teach the impact of your program on the business.

Leverage your presentation skills, and just as with any other project, eliminate the extraneous information and look to minimize cognitive load. For example, when you're folding in the data, surface it strategically so you don't overwhelm the listeners.

Daniel on Explaining Value to the C-suite

I remember that I once entered a meeting after completing a wide range of cohort analyses where I had found all of these strong correlations. I had data about the relationships between training and retention rates, training, and NPS and conversion rates — in fact, for almost every metric that I could find that mattered, I had found a strong correlation. I was so impressed by all the numbers, and I felt really validated that my work had such a strong impact. As a result, I threw everything into the presentation. There were so many numbers and insights in my slides that the presentation lost all shape, form, and structure. I had no clear narrative in what I was explaining, and from the executives' point of view, it was unclear how any of this mattered to the most pressing needs of the business; it was just a bunch of correlations. Looking back now, if I could do it again I would have chosen one or two metrics that told the story I wanted to tell and gone in with a single message. "I know that we're super focused on getting our product adoption numbers higher right now. Well, let me tell you what the numbers are saying about the relationship between training and product adoption."

Know Your Audience

It's important to think about what your audience needs to know. Think about three main audiences here, and segment the message accordingly.

Managers   Your manager needs to know the impact of your program so that they understand how your contributions impact the team. They want to see the benefit of your work, and they will often show interest in the details. Feel free to provide insight into the shapes and forms and colors involved in your story. Broaden the scope. Talk about the relationships between what you're doing and other departments in the business. Surface challenges and risks, and what you learned along the way. Make sure you can provide access to additional materials if managers request.

Executives   In contrast to your manager, executives are holding "the big picture" in mind and thinking about the relationship between multiple functions. They often need to prioritize in ways that can feel like a trade-off between priorities (investing more in one function than another, for example). Executives usually don't want to "zoom into" the details of what you're doing all day. Instead, they want to glean the overall significance and the conclusions of your program, and they want to hear how your work is connected to the current objectives of the business. Keep it sharp and simple, and don't overload them with information. One technique is to use a 1-2-3 rule – one overall point, two metrics or slides, and three minutes or less for the whole pitch.

Company   The third audience type is your company, and it often gets left out. Look for opportunities to evangelize education and help others to understand the value so that people can see the great work that your team is doing. While it's usually easy to see what sales and marketing are up to due to flashy campaigns, customer education can get a little lost in terms of recognition. This can work against you in a number of ways, especially when you're trying to get assistance from other teams. Think about how you can tell the story of what you've achieved to the wider company to help them understand the impact. One tip is to share quotes from customers that show how they perceive value, such as, "This training really gave me a lightbulb moment in terms of how to use the product to save time in my working day!"

Best Practices for Storytelling

Our brains crave a linear structure, so it shouldn't come as a surprise that when you tell a story, it should have a beginning, a middle, and an end.

However, sometimes it's tempting to come out with the data straightaway. Resist that impulse! If you're telling a good story, your data is the climax of the narrative and you need to build your way there. Start by laying the groundwork – what problem are you trying to solve? Remind everyone in the room why your education exists and what you're trying to do. Then explain what you did to help solve that problem, before coming in strong with the finding – 55 percent ROI, boom!

Make sure that you draw on emotion, as this is a really important part of storytelling. We have two sides to our brains, the logical side (which you've appealed to with your hard data), and the personal relationships side, which needs equal attention. Think about using quotes from customers to explain the challenge or the impact. Saying "We aren't getting wide usage of our product within single accounts" is much less impactful than saying "A customer said to me that they personally love using the product, but they have been having a huge problem getting other members of their team to change the way they work and give it a try." This really helps people to hear and understand the problem you're trying to solve.

Finally, it's important to give your audience a way to visualize the data by using clear, concise charts, graphs, or tables that bring the information to life. We had a really powerful moment recently at Thought Industries where we had successfully driven more traffic and engagement with our Academy. We created a chart that showed the daily engagement rate over time, both before and after we launched the new version of the Academy. It used a simple line and then clearly labeled the date of launch. At that point, the line takes a sharp swerve sky-high, showing in a single glance the impact of what we had achieved. We shared it with everyone with a simple caption: "Look what we did!"

Grab Your Seat at the Table

This is where our *Playbook* comes full circle. So many people that we speak to are craving growth. They want VP roles, and they want to be part of the conversation around strategy and change. However, they aren't mobilizing the customer education function to create the infrastructure they need to understand what ROI looks like for their company.

The good news is, you already know that managing the customer learning journey impacts every level of the business and every part of the customer experience. While this is a compelling story in and of itself, you don't get a seat at the table just because you think what you're doing is important. You need to earn it by demonstrating effectively how your function is contributing to profitability or to the margins of the company – and essentially, to the goals and challenges that everyone around that table is focused on right now.

So, back to step one we go. What is the goal of the business? Where is the organization feeling pressure? And how can you make sure that the goal of your customer education program aligns with that? With a sharp understanding of how these objectives align, you can demonstrate your impact effectively with both the data and the story, prove your worth as a vital function of the business, and take destiny into your own hands.

Read on for some additional best practices for using data to prove the ROI of customer education from Dave Derington, director of customer education at ServiceRocket, who formerly led Customer Education at Outreach.

Thoughts from . . . Dave Derington, Director of Customer Education, ServiceRocket

Every place in which I've been hired starts with a pain point that they're looking to solve. It could be an admin who struggles to set up a system, a user who is confused and churns because they don't know how to use the product, or a larger goal of low product adoption rates or poor retention, but the organization has a problem to solve in mind. The question for me is, how am I going to prove to an executive that my work matters – that education makes an impact on what they're looking to solve?

At the moment, I'm seeing more customer education openings than ever before in the job market. Everywhere I look, people are hiring for instructional and learning experience designers. The word has gotten out that customer education can provide value! There's a lot of FOMO (Fear of Missing Out) going on in leadership, where executives might not understand exactly what value they

(continued)

can achieve or what they are trying to influence, but they're often prone to jump in and start building out an educational program anyway. It's not always a bad thing to hit the ground running and just get some consumption happening around your content. After all, you can't prove ROI without the data, which you only get from creating the educational material. However, it doesn't work to jump in blind, either – you still need a process in place so that ultimately you can create that winning story around your impact.

Phase One: LMS Data

So, let's say you've been tasked by an executive to go out and build a customer education program and prove its value. Your C-suite is sold on starting the program, but you want to provide some data to show that the investment is worth it. Your first phase starts with creating a solid hypothesis that will fill the gap for what the customer needs to know. At Outreach, for example, the most common end user is a sales development representative (SDR). If Outreach has been purchased for them, their time to value (TTV) will be when they see they are able to put prospects into a sequence and begin to work on engaging with those prospects. Their lightbulb moment is when they see that Outreach will help them to do their work more effectively.

Now, don't forget to think about different personas (or cohorts). If you're talking about a power user or an administrator, they will have a different goal, and so the education needs a different focus, usually onboarding quickly or getting trained with initial usage. Once you've created learning around the right goal, put that education into your LMS, share and push the content to get people involved, and start tracking the consumption and sentiment around the education.

At this stage, you're not thinking about larger metrics such as impacting customer retention or adoption of the product. It's frustrating when leaders ask for that kind of data right off the bat, because you're not there yet! My job at this stage is simply to create content and then encourage customers to use it. When I can present a graphic that shows we've increased the monthly active users of the university by 250 percent over two years – perhaps augmented by satisfaction metrics like NPS or CSAT that also come from your LMS – that's going to get me a lot of smiles from the executives.

Phase Two: Connecting What You've Uncovered to the Wider Business

Most customer education teams that I've been a part of stop here. Especially if you're a fledgling company, you probably won't have the resources or infrastructure to go further than consumption and satisfaction, and that's okay. In my experience, many C-suites are happy with that. However, it doesn't mean you're absolved of the responsibility of looking to the next step.

If you can successfully combine the data from your LMS with your CRM data, support data, and other customer information, you can start tracking trends and begin to make correlations over time, using cohort analysis to compare trained and untrained accounts or users. At Gainsight, we were able to show that a typical onboarding would usually take 135 days to implement, but when a company had absorbed and paid for training, this reduced to just 36 days. When you put this on a dashboard, you're saying a few things. First, that a greater number of people are paying for training – that's direct revenue for the company. Second, that onboarding is getting easier for the customer – that's solving a pain point for the admin and the end-users. Third, you've saved 100 days of resources! Instead of focusing support and technical teams on onboarding this specific customer, your teams can quickly move onto the next, achieving serious efficiencies of scale.

This is a single metric, time to first value (or time to onboard), but you can do the same thing with product adoption rates,

(*continued*)

customer retention, NPS . . . you can really ask any question you want, connecting your LMS to Salesforce or Dynamics or HubSpot, and then use the data to show how training and education can move the needle. Your story becomes:

- "Companies who are taking training are retained at a higher rate than those who are untrained."
- "Our program has decreased churn by 15 percent since the relaunch of the Academy."
- "We've seen 70 percent fewer support tickets on this issue since we created an on-demand course."

So, ask yourself: What are you trying to influence with your education? And where can you find that data?

This brings us to the end of the 12 steps of the *Playbook* — a methodology for helping you develop, execute, and measure a customer education plan. But our research doesn't end there! In the next chapter, we will present our customer education maturity model, based on dozens of interviews with real-world customer education leaders in the field today. With this model, you can track your goals and progress against five distinct phases. These phases map out the success of your customer education journey as a function within the organization. We've also overlaid the steps of the *Playbook* where relevant, to support you with the challenges that you might face in achieving your own unique goals.

15 | Your Roadmap to High-Performance Customer Education

As part of our research into the state of customer education, and our charter of "educating the market," we spoke to dozens of organizations about their goals, their challenges, and the initiatives that helped them advance the performance of their programs. We identified the qualities of great customer education leaders, and we asked several of these leaders to share their journey, their insight, and their advice.

These stories highlighted the natural contours for how customer education programs evolve and thrive, and surfaced the unique obstacles faced by professionals in the field. Ultimately, we identified a five-stage roadmap from the earliest, least-mature programs all the way to those that are at the most innovative and future-focused stage of the game. You can see this maturity model in Figure 15.1. Now that we've reached the end of the *Playbook*, we want to share it with you as a reference and a guide for achieving growth in your own customer education programs.

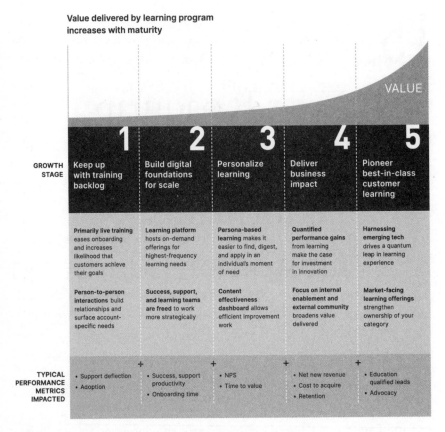

Figure 15.1 Customer Education Maturity Model

The Five-Stage Maturity Model for Customer Education

How can you use this maturity model? First, recognize that all companies will go through these stages, but not all at the same pace. Everyone starts at stage one, but some will quickly go from two to three – if, for example, they have comparatively more budget or buy-in from their executive teams. Others will stagnate at stage one or two for years, or even decades, before they recognize the importance of changing the way they approach customer education.

It's also important to recognize that the later stages in the maturity model are hard – and some might not even be possible yet for your organization. Rather than see the model as a race to the finish, consider the stages as a way to identify and address the challenges and goals that you're facing right now as a team, and what you can focus on for your own growth and success.

Stage One: Keeping Up with Live Training Needs

At stage one, training is predominantly live. Your instructors fly all over the world and offer education services or live training. If you're a SaaS company, your version of this might be customer success managers (CSMs) who solve challenges on the fly, answering tickets or helping customers to onboard or troubleshoot.

So, why do many organizations get stuck at stage one and never successfully launch a digital offering?

First off, there are some great things about this stage. Training is highly personalized, and human moments between your instructors and your customers help to build relationships and surface issues you might not have considered. Great training is both an art and an experience, and as a result, the engagement factor can be really high for your learners with stage one alone. For some niche companies, this might be exactly what's needed to get customers working with your offering.

More important still, moving forward takes substantial resources and time. You need to invest in a platform, learn how to use it and deploy it, onboard staff who understand eLearning, instructional design, or video design – it can be intense. The mental shift can also be a hard sell, because in a world of live training, every customer wants a bespoke offering, and they might push back against the change. If you can't see how you would achieve the same level of customization digitally, and your learners are getting a lot of value out of the status quo, why would you go through all the hard work of change management and moving away from person-to-person education?

Here's why. Every hour of training that you give is equal to an hour of your instructor's time, as well as all the additional work of preparation, delivery, and logistics. Even if an instructor doesn't need to prepare for a course they have given 100 times, they still need to physically get to the location and give over the information. Even if a CSM can answer an onboarding challenge in their sleep, you still need to hire more support reps if you get 50 more customers using the platform. Simply put, stage one is impossible to scale.

Stage Two: Laying a Digital Foundation for Scale

At stage two, you've invested time and effort in finding and implementing some kind of technology, and you're starting to create an on-demand offering for your customers. It can be slow. Maybe it's low-tech like YouTube videos or a podcast. However, it's helping you to build digital solutions for the education that your instructors or CSMs have been giving over and over again – your most common requests. From the customer's point of view, training is now delivered at the moment of need; they can search for the answer to a question or complete on-demand training when they start a new role or onboard your product. Your human interactions become more nuanced and strategy-focused, and live trainers stop saying the same things on repeat.

For everything that's positive about it, this stage is also a frustrating one. You might not have all the expertise you need, so you call on your instructors or support and success teams to help you create digital learning. These people already have a day job, and it's an important one! They're already working with customers all day, and there's a capacity crunch in asking them to do additional work, especially outside of their comfort zones.

Many customer education professionals brought up the challenge of an "infinite loop," where they finish updating their certification, eLearning course, or onboarding program, only to have to update it again immediately because of a change to the product. Chasing an infinite backlog means they rarely have the bandwidth to approach anything new.

Another challenge of phase two is that the education that you're creating is on-demand, but it's also one-size-fits-all. It fails to address the unique learning needs of all of your customers, instead focusing on the lowest common denominator (usually, this means a basic "101" style training). It's also usually not built with much expertise, as you're in unchartered territory. You don't know what good looks like yet. As a result, learners are faced with a six-hour course when they have a five-minute question, and you don't have a way to measure how customers are consuming or responding to what you're putting out there.

Stage Three: Making Learning More Personal and Easier to Consume

Stage three often starts with a segmentation strategy. You realize that your administrators need to know one thing, your engineers need another, marketing teams need a third, and so on, as we discussed when we talked about identifying learning personas. In stage two, you built for the demands of your business, but now you're looking to solve customer needs. You're starting to recognize the nuance in your learner base and understand what problems each of these categories of learners are trying to solve. Now you can build for these personas. Your offerings are becoming more diverse and modular; the format of your education may have changed from long recordings to shorter microlearning or perhaps in-app or in-product learning. The point is that you've optimized the format so it's more consumable.

As a result of all this work, by the end of phase three, individual users start feeling more supported and understood. You're building loyalty, and consumption improves.

At stage three, your main challenges are that you're still a siloed function in the organization. You might have an LMS that gives you data on consumption, but it's unlikely that you have data analytics tools in place to analyze your consumption data. You're starting to set goals, but it's tough to break the information you have down into something usable. If your data shows you that content is being consumed, that's all it tells you. There's no way to link that back to wider business goals or to prove the ROI of your program. You have a serious visibility and integration challenge. If your support teams want to work on ticket deflection, or your product team is planning a big update, you're two steps behind and playing catch up.

Stage Four: Delivering Business Impact

In stage four, you're shifting from customer impact to business impact, and from implying value to actually showing it. To reach stage four, you need to be connecting the dots of what the customer education function is doing to the rest of the business, like we discussed in Step 12 (Chapter 14) – proving ROI. Are you generating leads, increasing sales, or reducing churn? Are you speeding up time to value for the customer, or adding brand advocates to the organizational structure? The hallmark of stage four is that you have a way to measure the positive impact of education on the company at large. Education has become part of the business, not an add-on. There's a collaboration going on between departments, where the customer education team might be driving a project, but it involves input and support from everyone.

Your impact is giving you influence in the business, and you're being invited to join strategy-based conversations to make a case for further investment and growth. Your learning program starts to become a community hub. At Thought Industries we host roundtables, webinars, and our yearly conference, Cognition, where thought leaders from across the customer education field build relationships, network, and learn. You're teaching and reaching people through your education.

That's not to say there aren't challenges at this stage. It can be hard work to integrate systems to get all the data that you need. The data from your LMS will often live in a silo, elsewhere from what's in your CRM, accounting systems, support databases, or other necessary stores within the business.

When you do get a clear view of the data you need, you may not get the answers that you want. You could have come all of this way only to find that while your customers are consuming your education, it's not correlating with improved product adoption, reduced churn, or any other business goal you had in mind. What was once an accepted hypothesis, that "it's working," is no longer true, and now the pressure is on to improve. With more visible data on the impact (and success) of your program, you're being held to a higher standard to perform, so your failures are also more visible.

Another large challenge is global growth. Different locations have unique and diverse needs for how they want to be educated, and it can be a huge leap to move from a Western-focused education strategy to develop learning in new cultures and build an impactful global strategy.

Stage Five: Pioneering Best-in-Class Customer Learning

To be recognized as being in stage five of the maturity model, your organization needs to be productively leveraging new technologies and learning strategies to redefine the standard for the industry. You're achieving an increasingly personalized level of learning for the customer in the moment of need, and you've built a global learning strategy that can differentiate needs for various cultural requirements. You're using machine learning and integrated databases to pull in information from everywhere in the business, and you may already be working on advanced predictive capabilities that help ascertain what your customers need to learn. You are connecting members of your learning community to a wider ecosystem through digital credentials and certifications. Where relevant, you're using new and innovative mixed modalities, from in-app augmented reality (AR) to help train on machinery in the moment of need, to QR codes on the shop floor that pull up common pain points with products to learn pre-purchase.

You're a thought leader, an innovator, and you're leading your market category through education. Other organizations hold up your program as a model for what they hope to achieve. Congratulations! But watch out, the stakes are higher than ever before.

How Do Great Leaders and Mature Programs Approach Customer Education?

An interesting reality of the maturity model is that to get started, you need to be an expert in education, able to teach and engage the customer effectively and under constraints of time and resources. However, to get to stage four or five, you need to be able to run education like a business. The truth is, it's rare that people have these skills in equal measure. Success requires a village – hard in any case, but especially tough in customer education, where you often find yourself a team of one. You suddenly need to be an instructional designer, a charismatic speaker, an LMS administrator, a product manager, a content marketer, a data scientist, a business analyst, and more. It's a tall order! Throughout our research, we have found four common traits of the most mature customer education program leaders, which can help you to navigate your way to these heights:

1. They are sophisticated about encountering resistance.
2. They think backward.
3. They build an engine, not a backlog.
4. They orchestrate customer education as a whole-org strategy.

Great Customer Education Leaders Are Sophisticated about Encountering Resistance

Change management is job number one. At every phase of your maturity, you're going to come up against resistance, whether it's instructors who are scared about losing their job to "the machines," or grumpy product teams that don't want to share their roadmap. Make sure that you establish a shared vision with peer leaders and executive sponsors alike, making your case early and often so it's widely known. Don't try to ignore dissent or anxiety – address it clearly before it undermines your cause. When you experience success, shout about it! Share the win across departments, highlighting the input of others as vital in the process. We hope you've found examples of how to do this effectively throughout the *Playbook*.

Great Customer Education Leaders Think Backward

By starting with the outcome, these program leaders know where they are going. Narrow in on the business impact that you want to make and the needle you're looking to move. Then, segment your user base and the problems that education needs to solve in order to adjust that metric. If this still feels cloudy to you, head back to the first few steps of the *Playbook,* which address how to pick complementary goals for the education and the customer and work out how to start your program from the outcome you're looking to achieve.

Another benefit of starting with the outcome is that you can create a shared vision with the teams you'll ultimately need to collaborate with further down the line. This helps cement your shared purpose.

Great Customer Education Leaders Build an Engine, Not a Backlog

You want to be building a development engine, not a project backlog. If you keep churning out education products in a silo, you'll be constantly playing catch-up, trying to update existing education and unable to focus on what's next. Instead, successful leaders build their content creation into the product development process, as we discussed in steps five and six of the *Playbook.* They involve cross-functional players into the build, getting input and support from sales, product, marketing, customer success, engineering, and more. From the other direction, they are looped into whatever the product development process is, tagged on the product management dashboard, invited to the sprint meeting, and a member of a cross-functional dashboard for product development.

These leaders also work in an agile way, creating short, modular content and iterating and releasing often, working with time, scope, and budget rather than toward the idea of perfect.

Great Customer Education Leaders Orchestrate a Whole-Org Strategy

We've seen that successful customer education leaders set priorities for their education from the vantage point of other executives, recognizing that the support or product teams know best what customers are struggling with, or that marketing teams might be best placed to say what customers will need tomorrow. They therefore prioritize new content in a cross-functional way, building and iterating together, and use content across the company for additional use cases. A help video could be built to handle an in-app moment of friction for the product team, but would also be perfect to support CSMs in resolving tickets autonomously. If you want to remind yourself about how to create content with an emphasis on cross-functional input at each stage, review steps seven, eight, and nine of the *Playbook*.

By bringing the whole organization into the customer education fold, you solve the common challenge of your peers and executives not "getting" the way your world works, and increase the likelihood that you'll get buy-in for what you need, whether that's a recognition that you could do with more people, an understanding of the potential for a specific new technology, or concurrence with the necessity of greater investment to meet your goals. After all, your goals have become everyone's goals. In the final steps of the *Playbook*, you should have learned how best to approach assessing the success of your education for the customer and the business, as well as communicating ROI effectively.

Great customer education leaders innovate, always one step ahead of where the industry is going. In the next, and final, chapter, we will look at the future of customer education, and give you our thoughts on what to watch out for as the industry continues to evolve.

16 | Looking Ahead: The Future of Customer Education

When we think about where customer education is going, we need to acknowledge that as a discipline, we are experiencing rapid growth. Data from our *Customer Education Report 2021* indicates that 60 percent of customer education programs are planning to increase their investments by more than 30 percent, with 90 percent indicating expansion overall. As the discipline grows, especially at such a rapid pace, we're going to see a lot of change and a lot of trial and error as we work out best practices and where to focus our efforts and investments.

What's Fueling This Growth?

In 2020, the world experienced a pandemic, the impact of which continues today as we write this book. It would be impossible to deny that the pandemic has produced an urgency around delivering customer education in a way that is both scalable and virtual. For decades beforehand, the status quo for training customers had been regional trainers who go out to a customer site and train in person, but now that paradigm has shifted. And there is no going back.

While the previous method of training relied on regional teams who met regional needs through instructor-led training, an online training strategy requires companies to create a centralized function based on customer education. Classroom experiences are being replaced by virtual classrooms and self-study online materials. The entire education system is undergoing a tremendous change. In response, many companies are experiencing the constraints of getting the right tools in place, creating engaging virtual experiences, and translating classroom skills into effective online learning.

As we emerge from the pandemic, we believe that we will see a permanent shift in how companies view their strategy for training their customers. One element of this shift will come from the business and the benefits of a centralized, scalable customer education function that can deliver training globally through virtual self-serve or online channels. On the other side of the coin, customers will continue to shift their expectations around how they consume learning. They will demand delightful, engaging experiences that are accessible to them at their own pace and can be accessed anywhere.

As businesses scale their customer education function, growth will build on itself. Companies will realize that customer education is a way to do more than just drive product adoption and deflect support tickets, and they will uncover a growing awareness of how customer education influences the entire lifecycle, from generating leads and growing brand awareness through to developing advocates and evangelists.

We predict a convergence of teams who are thinking about the same kinds of outcomes and goals, from content marketing teams and education services to customer success and marketing departments. In some ways, all of these business functions have always been thinking about customer education and performing customer education–style tasks and activities. It therefore makes sense to see these departments align to a centralized function that coordinates learning across the lifecycle.

What Innovations Will Come Next for Customer Education?

When we think about innovation, we're not talking about the formation of creative ideas and blue-sky thinking. True innovation is not just something "cool," it's sustainable and long-lasting, and it comes from a place of "What needs fixing?" Innovation provides value by taking something that's difficult or a struggle right now, and working out a way to do it better, with less effort or greater accuracy. If you want to find a place for innovation, ask yourself, "Where is the struggle?" With that as our framework for discussion, let's think about the future of customer education and where innovation is set to thrive.

Beating the Challenge of Measurement

We've said multiple times across this *Playbook* that it is a universally felt challenge in customer education to understand the impact of the work that we do. It's not until we can solve the problem of data that we will be able to see a rapid acceleration of customer education as an essential function of the business. Until then, we are relying on the necessity of virtual training to meet the needs of a remote landscape and the innate knowledge that learning is a good thing to get us from one project to the next. We need to go beyond intuition and think about how we can provide hard data on how customer education is producing business results. That's how we will facilitate the creation of roles such as VP of customer education.

To measure and manage data more impactfully, we see the current model of delivering content via an LMS shifting to a new paradigm. Most learning management systems aren't built for the purpose of customer education – they are built for internal education or corporate training. As a result, they might have a lot of metrics on enrollment rates or completion rates, but almost nothing that can show the impact of education on the business.

Instead, consider the idea of a customer learning management (CLM) system that can connect the learning technology with other business systems and facilitate communication between them all. Imagine a platform powered by AI that analyzes your product data in one integrated system, including where customers are clicking and engaging, what support data is coming in through tickets, the search data and queries that your customers are inputting, and more. It then creates a report that recommends exactly what learning experience you need to create to address friction or meet a specific gap. In this reality, learning professionals can sign into their CLM and see at a glance the impact of their training on the business, looking at the effect of training on renewals or adoption in much the same way as sales can log into their CLM today and get the answers that they need. Up until now, when customer education teams have looked to understand impact, they have needed to go into multiple systems and piece it all together into a single story of potential correlations. In the future, we will see a far more streamlined and connected system for data from across the business, offering a single story from inside the customer learning system or platform.

While data will be a huge part of this journey, a CLM system will also help teams to improve and iterate their education and to figure out exactly where customers are struggling, eliminating the guesswork and manual effort that this has taken in the past. Instructional designers will be able to target their curriculum to pain points with greater ease, making education more effective as a whole.

Learning Anywhere

It should be obvious to anyone living in the modern era that learning has changed beyond recognition. What was previously a "you learn in a class-room" mentality has moved to the idea of learning anywhere. Although a person might have traditionally bought a book or signed up for a course, we now learn freely from multiple devices and across channels, including social media, internet news feeds, or even a YouTube rabbit trail. It has become universal to learn and consume in multiple places, and it's tough to imagine a world where we can't idly wonder about the answer to a question and look it up in moments from the device that is always at your fingertips.

Without the learning-anywhere mindset, customer education will quickly fall behind. While the status quo is currently an academy of learning experiences where your customer must leave their environment and go to a separate place to learn, this just isn't aligned with the learning-anywhere mindset. Instead, we predict a convergence of education in product – not just guiders but deep learning that promotes sustainable change and allows you to connect the dots and apply learning to novel situations.

Customer education programs will also need to expand beyond conventional channels to meet the needs of customers who are learning anywhere. We'll see more businesses launching YouTube channels, Twitter strategies, programs for delivering learning on Instagram or TikTok, and more. After all, if customers are learning anywhere, they will find information about your product on these channels – it just won't be from you. As we've established that creating an effective and engaging learning experience requires a strong skillset, you don't want to leave this up to an unknown YouTuber to handle on your behalf. In fact, that's the best way to end up with inaccurate or out-of-date information. For an optimal learning experience, more customer education programs will create a social media strategy of their own.

As part of this, you can expect augmented reality (AR) to play a larger role in contextual education for learning in areas such as manufacturing. While SaaS has played an outsized role in customer education up until now, many other industries have significant training needs, from medical devices to manufacturing, and as the paradigm moves from face-to-face instruction to online learning, it's not feasible to expect customers to pause in their use of products or machinery to go learn something on a computer or in an office and then go back to their role. AR can allow customer education to be delivered in person, at the moment of need, offering contextual, just-in-time education that supports the learner and opens up new verticals for customer education teams who are designing content.

The Development of an Agile Growth Mindset

As customer education grows and receives heavier investment, and as products themselves become more complex, professionals will need to get better at learning how to go to market with rapidly shifting and changing products. There will definitely be a trade-off here. We would hazard a guess that a lot of customer education professionals are currently spending more time and resources on learning experiences that make sense considering the pace of change. In the future, we will see a more agile mindset become the norm, moving away from the corporate L&D way of doing things where a piece of education can be used for many years to train on a specific or evergreen need. Instead, customer education teams will ask themselves, "What's the quickest way that I can put out something and get it in the hands of customers?" Since they know that it will quickly become obsolete, there is no need to spend too much time on it.

Innovation in this area will come in the form of mindsets and technology alike. While teams will spend less time producing eLearning courses and focus on quick wins like short videos, some companies are also innovating with new products that can use AI to automatically scan your product and create content that includes screencasts and simple content, freeing up customer education teams to add value elsewhere. Added benefits include the ability to automatically translate and localize content for different regions. It might not be the most sophisticated education content, but it can and will meet a quick need.

Changing Customer Expectations

An increasing number of customers want to be delighted by their vendors. Expectations are rising for consumer-grade learning experiences, and companies just aren't going to be able to get away with dry and boring content for much longer. Your customers will see that the competition is offering more modular, easier-to-consume content that is convenient, personalized, often in-context, and highly focused on their needs.

If appropriate for your industry, it is likely that you'll also see a move to a lighter touch for educational content, incorporating humor and fun where possible. This holds greater appeal for younger audiences, who often have the majority of the buying power and are heavily swayed by stellar digital experiences.

Customers are already looking toward their vendors for not just product training but also skills training. Think about opening a new blender and, as well as being provided with instructions for how to use the machine, you're given a pamphlet or a QR code that offers recipes on how to make great smoothies. Ultimately, the customer bought the blender to make delicious food – that's the job it was hired to do – and the company is serving that need by showing you how to use their tool to meet that outcome.

When we think about the future of customer education, customers will expect certifications and credentials that will largely displace the idea of going back to school to learn a new skill. Instead of pursuing a data analysis degree, customers will look to your company for a data analyst course that can help them to upskill and reskill, and that offers a certification or a digital credential that can help them to get the job they want. This will fall into the laps of companies who will be expected to offer this skills training and will also provide benefits to the business as they become synonymous with their market, in a similar way to HubSpot or Salesforce.

As companies certify and train more users, this will trigger another result. With the help of certified experts who know the product and its value inside and out, customer education teams will establish more reach with advocates who can be crowdsourced to create content on your behalf. This ultimately feeds into a growth loop that supports immense opportunities for scale.

It All Starts and Ends with . . . Customer Education Strategies

Perhaps the most important thing that's happening in the world of customer education right now, while we're experiencing this rapid and record growth, is that more and more businesses are becoming strategic about their approach. This is a new discipline, and yet we're already seeing so many companies move from being reactive about education to being firmly proactive about the direction they want to take.

There is now a real recognition of the value of having a framework and a plan in place, understanding the learning journey of the customer, and orchestrating education so that customers are learning the right thing at the right time. Once this mindset has been fully adopted and we're wholly focused as a discipline on a convergence of strategies for how to demonstrate value and develop effective and engaging content, we expect to see exponential growth in our programs. We hope this book can be a catalyst for that growth.

Acknowledgments

From Daniel:

Writing a book has always been a dream of mine, and I have many people to thank who helped make this dream come true. First and foremost, thank you to my co-author Barry Kelly, for placing your faith in me, and for your commitment to empowering the customer education community. It's invigorating to work for a CEO who is so invested in the success of our customers and the growth of our industry.

I am so lucky to have Adam Avramescu as my mentor and my friend. Adam, thank you for inviting me to join your team many years ago, and for setting me on this journey in customer education. You are an inspiration to me and so many others in this industry.

I've had the pleasure and privilege of working with many amazing colleagues who have shaped my perspective in this field. While I can't list them all, I want to give special thanks to Yeesheen Yang, Wes Richards, Melissa Muñoz, Kaitie Chambers, Maggie Coffin, Carla Bagdonas, Paul Merrylees, Brian Childs, and Sandra Elliott. I hope each of you will recognize your own contributions in the stories I've shared here.

Early in the process of writing this book, I realized how important it was to include the perspectives of customer education leaders whose work exemplifies excellence. For donating their time and sharing their thoughts, I am grateful to Adam, Eric Peters, Lisa Rothrauff, Debbie Smith, Bill Horzempa, Dee Kapila, Melissa VanPelt, Michelle Wiedemer, Alessandra Marinetti, Tom Studdert, Cary Self, and Dave Derington.

I am also so thankful for the many people in my life who have supported and encouraged me along the way, especially my three pillars. My mom, who unwaveringly believes I can achieve anything I put my mind to. My twin brother, who gives me unconditional love and acceptance. And my husband, who helps me realize the best possible version of myself.

Finally, I want to thank the team at Wiley for recognizing the importance of customer education, and give my deepest gratitude to Elisheva Sokolic for gracing us with her writing talents. I feel so fortunate to have crossed paths with you.

From Barry:

I want to first and foremost thank my amazing wife, Julie, who has been the most exceptional partner on this exciting and sometimes grueling journey of building a software company from the ground up. Your support, pep-talks, advice, and love have made it all worthwhile. To my incredible kids, Fionn and Niamh, who inspire me and keep me smiling no matter how tough the day is. To my parents back in Ireland, Ned and Kay, who gave me an amazing upbringing and made so many sacrifices for me, and from whom I learned the most important value: work ethic. I am so grateful. To Daniel, who worked so tirelessly on this book. You have been an amazing co-author and colleague and your passion for our industry is unrivaled.

Thanks so much to Paul, Kathleen, Susie, and Peter for your belief, support, and family friendships that I cherish. To the founding team at Thought Industries: Doug Murphy, John Danner, and Chris McClelland, what a journey it has been together! To the current Thought Industries management team, all of whom I am fortunate to call friends: Robin Wadsworth, Rob Lubash, Sam Bourneuf, Sarah Camacho, Todd Boes, Mike Daecher, Therese Kelleher, Mike Jahoda, David Downing, Eleanor Young, and John Tegan. Our board: Chris Murphy, Hollie Haynes, Dave Ulrich, and the super team at Luminate Capital. To Jon Guido and Doug Hurst and the team at AGC. To those of you who have made the journey from the start at Thought Industries: Ryan Dillon, Andrei Kharazia, Dave Riely, and Brittany Ross, your loyalty and commitment has made a huge difference. A special thanks to Paul Iannacchino, Billy Cole, and Jane Goldman, who believed in the vision early and helped us make it happen.

To my close friends (and band mates) who make being on this planet all the better: Angela Dorgan, Mike Coen, Paul O'Flynn, Ciaran Cusack, Matt Diekmann, Dave Franz, Hugh Buchan, David and Iain McDonald, Kev Greely, and too many more to mention.

To our early customers who believed in the vision, helped us carve a path, and stuck in: Tad Goltra, Winter Thielen, Tom Studdert, David Katzman, Karen Swindells, Gary Charlton, Scott Miller, Russ Rollins, and so many more. To our partners at Service Rocket: Rob, Bill, and Mel. To the many folks who lead this industry with your thought leadership: John Leh, Adam Avramescu, Dave Derrington, Maria Manning-Chapman, Craig Weiss, Donna Webber, Bryan Chapman, and to great organizations such as CEDMA and TSIA.

I also want to acknowledge everyone that makes up this amazing industry of customer, partner, and professional education. I am inspired daily by the work you do and look forward to a day when the topic of customer education is present in every boardroom.

Finally, thanks so much to Elisheva Sokolic and the team at Wiley for your support and guidance in bringing our customer education framework to the world.

About the Authors

Daniel Quick has been on the front lines of customer education, creating results-driven customer learning and brand-building thought leadership at leading software brands, including Optimizely, Asana, and Thought Industries. He is passionate about delighting customers and helping them achieve success through learning.

Barry Kelly is co-founder and CEO of Thought Industries, the #1 customer training platform. He is a champion of the customer learning industry and has worked with hundreds of professionals to deliver impactful training experiences that keep customers engaged and renewing over time.

Index